US
and Yet
and Yet

together we rise

beyond traditional roles

Josee Tremblay

© Josee Tremblay 2024. All rights reserved.

No part of this book may be reproduced in any form or by any means without written permission from the publisher.

Editor: Kim Farnell

Cover Design: Farrukh Khan

Cataloging-in-Publication Data is on file with the Library and Archives of Canada

ISBN 978-1-0689573-0-7 (Hardcover) ISBN 978-1-0689573-1-4 (Paperback Book)

ISBN 978-1-0689573-2-1 (EBook)

To my biggest ally, my spouse Colin, with whom I enthusiastically share my life, a son, and a daughter.

The world of dew—
A world of dew it is indeed,
And yet, and yet..."
露の世は露の世ながらさりながら
tsuyu no yo wa tsuyu no yo nagara* sari nagara.

Kobayashi Issa

Thank you for buying my book. Find free high impact material to support your diversity journey at www.usandyet.com

Contents

Foreword 1

Introduction 4

Chapter 1.
The Business Case for Allowing our World to be Shaken 9

Chapter 2.
Finding Power in Archetypes 27

Chapter 3.
Nurturing Equal Partnerships 61

Chapter 4.
Embracing and Enabling Diversity in Business and at Home 77

Chapter 5.
Balancing Act: Work, Family, and Gender Expectations. It's a societal project for men and women. 102

Chapter 6.
Effective Communication Across Diversity Lines 122

Chapter 7.
Thriving Together: Participative Decision-Making . 133

Chapter 8.
Resolving Conflict and Negotiating Empowering Solutions 143

My Story.
Love the people you work with and the people you
live with even more 160

Afterword.
Celebrating Diversity and Individual Achievements
.... 172

Let's get inspired! 175

References.. 176

Foreword

US and yet and yet: together we rise beyond traditional roles

The phrase "US and yet and yet" can be unpacked to reveal a variety of philosophical implications, particularly when considered in the context of identity, existence, and contradiction. From a point of view of identity and multiplicity, the "US" can be interpreted as a collective, representing a group or society. The repetition of "and yet" suggests continual questioning or re-evaluating of this identity. Philosophically, this reflects a state of complexity and fluidity. It acknowledges that even as we form a cohesive "US", there are always elements that challenge and redefine that unity. But what collective identity has the highest chance of lifting our hearts and making us proud to leave for the next generation? One that leaves no one behind.

Through the lens of existence and paradox, the title phrase explores societal enigma and contradiction.

While we might wish to leave no one behind, the reality is we've tried and we've failed, or made little progress, and we don't know what to try next. This lens brings the "US" under the spotlight as being in a state of existence rather than growth, while "and yet and yet" implies an opportunistic state of becoming or change for the better. This resonates with the ancient Greek philosophy of Heraclitus, which posits that everything is in flux and we can never step into the same river twice. The essence of "US" is, as a result, seen as non static and constantly evolving.

In a dialectical sense, "US and yet and yet" symbolizes the ongoing tension between thesis and antithesis, where "US" is the thesis, and "and yet and yet" represents the antitheses or the challenges and contradictions that continuously arise. This aligns with Hegelian dialectics, where the synthesis is an ever-evolving process driven by the resolution of contradiction.

From an existential viewpoint, the phrase emphasizes the perpetual search for meaning and self-understanding. "US" denotes our current understanding or state, while "and yet and yet" suggests there is always more to uncover, more layers to our existence, and more questions than answers. It highlights the never-ending quest for self-discovery and the acceptance of uncertainty. Discovering the unconscious biases that impede our progress is essential on our journey towards empowerment and self-actualization.

In postmodernist philosophy, which often deconstructs notions of absolute truths and stable identities, "US and yet and yet" can be seen as a critique of any definitive claims about identity. It underscores the fragmented, de-centered, and constantly contested nature of our understanding of "us." What if we rose above this pain of dissonance and heart disenchantment and felt the joy and pleasure of succeeding together?

In summary, "US and yet and yet" signifies the dynamic, ever-changing, and complex nature of our collective and its existence. It highlights the contradictions and ongoing processes of becoming that define who we are, both individually and as a global society, and ultimately what we choose to do with that potential.

This book provides insights on fostering gender equality, prioritizing relationships, and achieving harmony between work and personal life. It will help empower you to navigate the complexities of modern life by forging a society beyond matriarchy and patriarchy, both in business and personal spheres.

Introduction

There's a society in our collective future that will maximize everyone's potential for greater happiness, health, and prosperity. Our societal efficiency in harnessing our power is far from optimal. By moving in alignment with our passions, we'll create a spark to ignite us all to our best potential. This book will delve into this vision in a way you might not have thought of before. It will free your mind from resistance and insecurity and transform your vision for the future.

Indeed, we need a collective vision. We need to be taken by the impulse to advance from where we are today and take targeted and informed actions in our respective ecosystems. This will advance our society, and we'll feel this momentum together in an irresistible way.

There's been a seismic shift in gender dynamics that's reshaping our professional and personal lives. Because everyone's work and home lives are inevitably intertwined, pulling and pushing for space in our day-to-day lives, I'll share some of my experiences in both. We'll look at barriers to overcome and means to enable us to arrive at this vision where our society is sophisticated enough to navigate the seismic shift in gender dynamics to foster inclusivity, equality, and success in an authentic and invigorating way.

We should all want this vision to materialize because gender equality is a key arsenal and strategic advantage in today's interconnected world.

In a reimagining of Martin Luther King Junior's iconic speech "I Have a Dream" on August 28, 1963:

I have a dream that one day gender won't be a barrier to opportunity and equality. I dream of a world where individuals are judged not by their gender, but by their character and the merits of their actions. Let's rise above the limitations of stereotypes and prejudices, embracing a future where every person, regardless of gender, can pursue their aspirations freely and without discrimination. Together, let's strive for a society where gender equality isn't just a dream, but reality for all.

We've made tremendous progress in recent decades in creating more inclusive societies, but we still have a long way to go. There's excitement and anticipation that comes from envisioning a world that's neither matriarchal nor patriarchal, but one that gives authority to those humble, wise, and compassionate enough to improve our collective quality of life and prosperity. While this book focuses on enabling opportunities for both men and women, it will provide insights for any group or individual in a minority environment.

Let's look at the gender construct itself. There is a remarkable movement underway whereby a distinction is made between a person's biological sex and the gender with which they identify. This book is centered around gender of identity. The segment about archetypes provides insight to help with applying the solutions and tools proposed to combat inequality and challenges, and to maximize everyone's potential regardless of their biological sex at birth.

In addition to archetypes, at the root of everything, from the subatomic particles that form the building blocks of matter to the colossal structures like superclusters and cosmic filaments that span vast distances across the universe, every scale offers a glimpse into the wonders of the positive and negative coming together in a bond. The phenomenon also holds true in non-physical domains. This energetic polarity is at the center of a lot of clues on the path to finding solutions to inequality.

We are at the dawn of seeing great momentum in the advancement of equality, but like every evolution, it's often two steps forward and one step back. There will be tension, unstable ground, and discomfort until we reach an equitable world sustainably. Ultimately, enabling sustained peace and happiness and better relationships between nations by eliminating inequity, finding more compassion for people with diverse views and tapping into a vast array of ideas that aren't currently given a voice or platform. The advancement will require us all to contribute, no matter what our gender, to reap its benefits. It is with a collective assessment, one of active and continuous learning, and of sharing of experiential knowledge that the long-lasting evolution towards maximizing the potential of our nations will take place. This book will cover:

- **Gender equity in business:** Achieving equal opportunities for career advancement and leadership roles regardless of gender.

- **Harmonious work-life integration:** Balancing professional success with personal fulfillment and meaningful relationships.

- **Effective communication:** Developing communication skills to navigate gender dynamics confidently.

- **Empowerment:** Feeling empowered to tackle gender norms and navigate gender equality in both personal and professional spheres.

- **Creating inclusive environments:** Fostering inclusive workplaces and communities where individuals are valued for their contributions regardless of gender.

In the global north, as in many other parts of the world, the patriarchal societal construct is strong and alive. Changing this reality not to swing it over to matriarchal, but to find a balance where the transformation is just enough to enable everyone to reach their full potential, will propel the US to unprecedented heights.

Chapter 1

The Business Case for Allowing our World to be Shaken

The person who figures out how to harness the collective genius of the people in their organization is going to blow the competition away.

Walter Wriston, Former Chairman of Citigroup[1]

When it comes to intention, the inclusion scenery has changed and evolved. While there's a consensus we want more, many of us are disappointed by the success rate of our efforts to date. It's important to assess current facts about why we should continue to care about helping the transition to a world that leverages all to their best potential.

Through the business lens, of course I want to help our society move in the direction of equality for everyone's greater happiness, but I understand that what moves much of the world is a thirst for prosperity. Prosperity brings the freedom to pursue what you love, and that's an attractive proposition for most.

I had the pleasure last year of attending a conference and meeting Karen Greenbaum at the Association of Executive Search and Leadership Consultants. She shared a white paper on International Women's Day 2024 titled "Unlocking the $172 trillion gender dividend."[2] Many of the statistics and findings in this chapter are sourced from this paper.

The World Bank study which published this conclusion, is exactly about what this book is trying to unleash: the untapped potential of all of us reaching for the best version of ourselves. Not a version that's distorted into someone else, or a version that's given up because of barriers or conflicting priorities, but a version that's full of life and stamina because there's thriving and passion in action. The World Bank paper highlights that if women were earning as much as men, human capital wealth could increase by about one fifth globally.[3] Gains would differ between regions and countries, but for the 141 countries included in the analysis, the total gain in human capital wealth from gender equality is estimated at US$172.3 trillion in 2017—US$24,586 per person.

	2000	2005	2010	2014	2017
Human capital wealth per capita, men	60,940	60,980	62,672	66,832	68,717
Human capital wealth per capita, women	35,538	36,727	39,498	41,823	42,852
Ratio of women vs men's human capital	58%	60%	63%	63%	62%
Loss of share of baseline human capital	26%	24%	22%	22%	18%
Loss of share of baseline wealth	18%	16%	14%	14%	(b)
Loss in human capital wealth per capita [a]	24,603	23,391	22,068	23,620	24,586

Figure 1: Human capital wealth by gender[4]

Notes: Given that gender inequality affects individuals throughout their life, economic costs are measured in terms of losses in human capital wealth, as opposed to annual losses in Gross Domestic Product (GDP) or GDP growth.

(a) To compute the potential losses in human capital wealth due to gender inequality, we simply estimate how much more human capital wealth countries would have if women were earning as much as men.

(b) Estimates for 2017 were based on projections and total wealth figures were not yet available at the time the source was published.

The sad part about this report is its highlight that globally we're losing ground and momentum. This loss of momentum should serve as a call to action, following the great lesson of one of my favorite short films from Pixar, *Boundin'* (2003), where after loosing their wool for the first time and being left barren, the sheep learns to dust themself off and stop getting fazed by adversity.

While these figures on human capital wealth are a few years old now, precision isn't the point here. The takeaway is the value is huge, and we'd be crazy not to want to help humanity tap into this opportunity. The methodology used in this estimation has many simplifications, but overall it aims to quantify the impacts of gender inequality on development outcomes and the economic costs associated with these potential impacts. My hypothesis is that this is a gap and not a transfer of human capital from one gender to the other. The power and bond that's forged by putting men and women together to create new heights of world performance, regardless of geopolitical boundaries, is the propulsion engine that has sub-optimally been capitalized on. This collective venture touches us all and harnesses and enables access to smarts and abilities which we, as a society, are underutilizing. We've seen it in our recent history. Based on a true story, one of the best movies on the subject is *Hidden Figures* (2016) about women mathematicians who played crucial roles at NASA during the early years of the United-States' space program. Wow, how powerful it is to see both genders tackle complex problems together and gain appreciation for each other's contributions!

This hypothesis that different alliances will create different outcomes is illustrated in my own life experience when I compare my first and second spouses. I was in a long-term relationship early in my life and appreciated the intellectual pursuits and analytical mind of my first spouse, yet my alliance with him didn't support my life pursuits. For example, while I was offered a great development role, which required a move for a period, he only accepted the move reluctantly and throughout the assignment was more focused on his needs than on us working together as a team. Our dynamic together didn't create a momentum toward a happy and prosperous future.

Fast forward a few years and with my new spouse, I found my match and the encouraging, caring support I needed to thrive. The difference in the alliances' outcomes is striking. We travel and have lived around the world as a dual-income couple, share two children, and constantly help each other grow; supporting each other in our passions. The relationship isn't just 50% different from my previous but 200%! The union of two people, and what we nurture, influence, and bring out is wildly different. This might seem obvious, but pausing to acknowledge how much our behavior and approach influences each other's success is of tremendous significance when it comes to diversity.

The reason why the relationship is so different is that there's a dynamic between the two elements of the equation that results in something greater (or worse) than the other association. Simply said, synergy changes influence the dynamic of a relationship and how we feel and are in it.

Today, we're on a phenomenal journey together, and I can truly feel we are the support we need to succeed. With the complementary nature of men and women in our society, if the elements of association are there to intentionally empower both sides, the sky's the limit as to what's possible to create in a positive climate. This is true for both our personal and professional lives.

A great model to go by on this journey of enablement is Kim Cameron's *Four Leadership Strategies to Enable Positive Deviance*.[5] In this simple and effective model, individuals and organizations produce life-giving and flourishing outcomes when organizational strategies are based on the positive. It's similar to the *heliotropic effect*—the movement of plants and flowers towards the sun's rays.

Cameron says:

In sum, positive leadership refers to an emphasis on what elevates individuals and organizations (in addition to what challenges them), what goes right in organizations (in addition to what goes wrong), what is life-giving (in addition to what is problematic or life-depleting), what is experienced as good (in addition to what is objectionable), what is extraordinary (in addition to what is merely effective), and [ultimately] what is inspiring (in addition to what is difficult or arduous). Leaders significantly affect organizational climate as they personally induce, develop, and display positive emotions.[6]

All our associations, whether at work or at home, consist of a dance between interacting entities. While it might be more comfortable to associate with our own gender, the rewards of embracing discomfort of association with a broader more diverse group are tremendous and can lead to heights we never thought possible before.

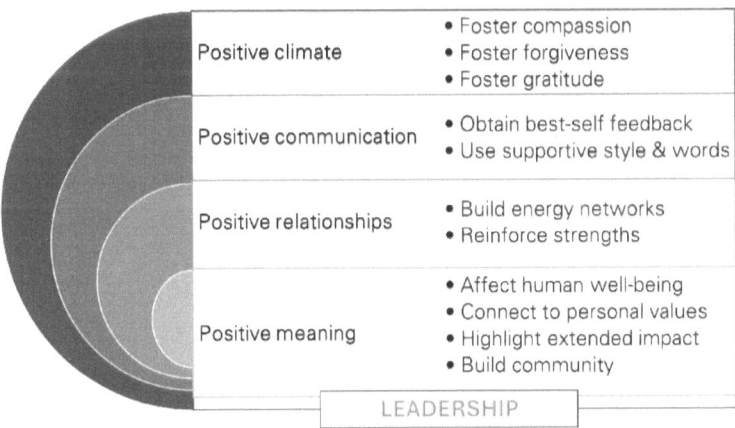

Figure 2: Four leadership strategies that enable positive deviance[7]

A brief description of the leadership strategies intrinsic to the concentric diagram is as follows: Research concludes that inducing positive emotions "broaden people's momentary thought-action repertoires and builds their enduring personal resources." Conversely, "negative emotions narrow people's thought-action repertoires and diminish their coping abilities."[8]

So, what are the documented advantages of luminous associations, those that are brilliant intellectually, enlightened or enlightening?

- **Enhanced creativity and innovation**
    - Diverse teams bring people together with different backgrounds, experiences, and perspectives. This diversity of thought leads to more creative problem-solving and innovative ideas.
    - When individuals from different walks of life collaborate, they can generate unique solutions that a homogenous group might not have considered.

- **Improved decision-making**
    - Diverse teams tend to make better decisions. They consider a wider range of viewpoints and potential risks.
    - Cognitive diversity, or differences in how people approach problems, can lead to more robust decision-making processes.

- **Better problem-solving**
    - Diverse groups can tackle complex problems more effectively because they draw from a broader pool of knowledge and skills.
    - Different perspectives allow for a more comprehensive analysis of issues, leading to better solutions.
- **Increased adaptability**
    - Organizations that embrace diversity are better equipped to adapt to changing environments.
    - Diverse teams can respond more flexibly to market shifts, technological advancements, and other disruptions.
- **Attracting and retaining talent**
    - When employees feel valued and respected, they are more likely to stay with an organization.
- **Market relevance and customer understanding**
    - Diverse teams can better understand and serve diverse customer bases.
    - In a globalized world, businesses benefit from having employees who can relate to and connect with customers from various cultural backgrounds.

- **Financial performance**
    - Research suggests that companies with diverse leadership teams tend to outperform their peers financially.
    - A study by McKinsey found that companies in the top quartile for gender diversity on their executive teams were 25% more likely to have above-average profitability.[9]

Diversity alone isn't enough; inclusion is equally crucial. Inclusion ensures that everyone's voice is heard and respected, creating a truly collaborative and effective environment that can reap the benefits, and outweigh the potential initial discomfort of associating with people who are not like us.

In recent years, many have come out with great stories about turnarounds in their company performance from embracing diversity. An example is that of Qantas. In 2013 it posted a record loss of AUD$2.8 billion.[10] This low point in the airline's 98-year history followed record-high fuel costs, the grounding of its A380s in 2010 for engine trouble, and the suspension of its entire fleet for three days in 2011 after a series of bitter union disputes. Across the country, predictions surrounding the fate of Australia's national carrier were dire.

Fast-forward to 2017, and the situation couldn't be more different. Qantas delivered a record profit of

AUD$850 million, increased its operating margin to 12 percent, won the "World's Safest Airline" award, ranked as Australia's most trusted big business and its most attractive employer, and delivered shareholder returns in the top quartile of its global airline peers and the ASX100. Transformation is an overused word, but for Qantas it's a perfect description. How did it happen? The company's 2017 Investor Roadshow briefing sounded like a textbook in disciplined operational and financial management, as well as employee, customer, and shareholder focus. Yet for CEO Alan Joyce, the spectacular turnaround reflects an underlying condition. He said, "We have a very diverse environment and a very inclusive culture." Those characteristics, according to Joyce, "got us through the tough times... diversity generated better strategy, better risk management, better debates, [and] better outcomes."[11]

With that much latent potential, figures indicate there is much more work to do to continue to challenge our biases and remove impedance to our progress towards diversity. As an example, according to 2023 data released by Washington-based non-partisan think tank, Pew Research Center, women made up just over 10% of CEOs in Fortune 500 companies, while the percentage of women who sit on the boards of those companies is 30.4%, which is on a par with the percentage of women who head up colleges and universities (32.8%). Despite some important gains in political leadership and government roles, there is a sense the status quo is not working and more needs to be done specifically on gender parity as a means to strengthen communities, economies and workplaces.[12]

The business case for women in the boardroom

In the last few years, I've been involved in and developed my expertise as a non-executive director in boardrooms. Leveraging my years of experience leading large organizations in industrial settings is one way of helping inspiring CEOs and executives to win in their pursuits. In addition, while I take a lot of pride in being highly adaptive, I'm conscious and aware that I bring a different perspective to the various tables. Being a minority in the room often comes with the realization that I may not interpret, see the world, or react to circumstances in the same way as others. This is part and parcel of diverse environments. The tables who figure out how to leverage this are a somewhat rare commodity in the non-traditional fields I find myself in, and are the ones which are welcoming, inclusive, considerate, humble, and where egos are checked at the door.

Last year, I was involved with a side project where senior executives of various sectors from pharmaceuticals to aerospace came around the room to solve a business dilemma. It was an intense two weeks, and in the middle of it we had to share our experiences with each other to help improve our performance in the following week. One of my colleagues described me as the "chemical equalizer" of the group. The other gentlemen in the room nodded in agreement and that made me smile. I was the only woman at the table, and they all felt I brought something different: a sense of grounding, clarity, and unity.

There was an interesting study published in 2024 by the *International Journal of Disclosure and Governance* called "Unpacking women's power on corporate boards: gender reward in board composition."[13]

Since 2004, when the UN Global Compact Initiative's "Who Cares Wins" report was published, the term *ESG* (environment social and governance) has been an integral part of our modern vocabulary.[14] This is particularly true in the vocabulary of the boards of publicly traded companies competing to attract increasingly demanding and more sophisticated investors. The jury is still out on whether it creates a true competitive advantage in some of financial metrics such as Return on Capital Employed directly or indirectly. One thing is for sure though, the shareholders' thirst for corporate sustainability performance has been increasingly present.

In the *International Journal of Disclosure and Governance*'s paper, the methodology was to capture data from nineteen European countries, having 2640 firm-year (where firm-year = [*total number of firms(N) mul-*

tiplied by sample period (t)) of observation, described correlation parameters of women on boards (WoB) versus a variety of metrics. Because the data is presented stochastically, it offers insights other articles don't. In particular, the study quantifies a minimum threshold for women on boards to have an impact on outcomes.

The data shows that WoB positively and significantly affect corporate sustainability performance at the 1% significance level where correlation coefficients normalized for random effects is greater than 0.251. In addition, the R-square of the model resulted in a coefficient of 39% described as significantly correlated in the statistical context, which indicates the instruments' adequate explanatory power.[15] In other words, it implies that better sustainability performance can be achieved when there's gender diversity in the boardroom. It's important to note that the study also highlights that women on boards start positively affecting corporate sustainability performance at a threshold of approximately 30%, ensuring synergetic impact.[16]

Another classic of the last decade is the *Deloitte Insights* article "The diversity and inclusion revolution: eight powerful truths."[17] It references Juliet Bourke's article "Which two Heads are Better than one? How Diverse Teams create Breakthrough ideas and make Smarter Decisions."[18] The value of diversity of thinking is pegged as increasing innovation by 20% and reducing risk by 30%.

Deloitte also tracks the progress of gender parity on boards around the world. A global perspective finds that women hold less than one-quarter of the world's board seats (23.3% in 2023) and that gender parity on boards will be elusive without greater focus and action. Globally, the percentage of women chairing boards is nearly three times lower than the percentage of women serving on boards, with just 8.4% of the world's boards being chaired by women.

Why should we care?

Key findings from research on the impact of gender diversity in boardrooms on company performance in the United States include:

- Studies have shown a positive correlation between gender-diverse boards and financial performance. Companies with greater gender diversity in their boardrooms tend to outperform those with less diverse boards in terms of financial metrics. Not all financial metrics are consistent and the importance of continuing to unpack what minimum thresholds of diversity is required to consistently make an impact is necessary.

- Gender-diverse boards are often associated with increased innovation and better decision-making processes. Diverse perspectives and experiences brought by women board members can lead to more creative problem-solving and a wider range of strategic options being considered.

- Gender diversity in boardrooms is linked to improved corporate governance practices and better risk management. Boards with diverse compositions are more likely to engage in effective oversight, reducing the likelihood of corporate scandals and governance failures.

- Companies with gender-diverse boards may experience higher levels of employee engagement and retention. Employees tend to perceive organizations with diverse leadership teams as more inclusive and equitable, leading to greater job satisfaction and loyalty.

- Gender diversity in boardrooms can enhance a company's reputation and brand image, especially among socially conscious consumers and investors. Organizations that prioritize diversity and inclusion in their leadership ranks may attract a broader customer base and enjoy stronger brand loyalty.

- Gender diversity in boardrooms can help companies comply with legal and regulatory requirements related to diversity and corporate governance. Many jurisdictions have introduced regulations or guidelines promoting gender diversity in corporate leadership, and companies that embrace diversity are better positioned to meet these obligations.

Correlation analyses typically aim to quantify the relationship between gender diversity in boardrooms and various performance metrics, such as financial indicators or market outcomes. These analyses often use statistical methods to assess the strength and direction of the relationship between gender diversity and company performance, controlling for other factors that may influence outcomes. While correlations may vary across studies, the overall evidence suggests a positive association between gender diversity in boardrooms and company performance. However, it's essential to interpret correlation findings cautiously and consider potential confounding variables that could affect the results.

> ## Chapter summary
>
> - **Genderquake[19] phenomenon:** In today's shifting landscape, diversity is a key driver of prosperity and fulfillment where embracing diversity isn't just about doing what's inspiring; it's about tapping into untapped potential for greater human capital wealth globally.
> - **Loss of momentum:** Despite strides made, recent trends suggest we're losing ground in the journey towards gender equality. But rather than succumb to despair, let's heed the call to action. Just as the Pixar short film *Boundin'*

teaches resilience in the face of adversity, this loss of momentum should galvanize us to push harder for progress.
- **Diversity and innovation:** Diversity isn't just a buzzword; it's the cornerstone of innovation. Drawing inspiration from transformative stories like *Hidden Figures*, we see how diverse teams bring fresh perspectives, driving creativity and unlocking solutions that were previously unimagined.
- **Positive leadership**: Leadership sets the tone for organizational climate, and positive leadership is the catalyst for success. By fostering environments where positivity thrives, we create fertile ground for innovation, collaboration, and ultimately, success.
- **Case studies and research**: Real-world examples like Qantas' remarkable turnaround underscore the tangible benefits of diversity. Backed by research findings, we see clear correlations between gender diversity in boardrooms and improved financial performance, innovation, and corporate governance.

In essence, this chapter underscores a simple truth: embracing diversity isn't just the inspirational thing to do—it's the smart thing to do. It's about recognizing the immense value that comes from harnessing the power of diverse perspectives and experiences, propelling us towards a future of unparalleled success and fulfillment.

Chapter 2

Finding Power in Archetypes

Love is the recognition of oneness in a world of duality.

Eckhart Tolle[20]

To unleash the potential of all, we have to be concerned with how our work and our personal lives intertwine. Becoming aware of the power in archetypes is fundamental to achieving success in both, and as a result sweepingly advancing diversity.

The word *archetype* was used by the Swiss psychologist Carl Jung in the early twentieth century to describe collectively inherited unconscious ideas, patterns of thought, and images universally present in individual psyches. Jung believed that archetypes come from the collective unconscious. He suggested that these models are innate (unlearned), hereditary, and universal. Jung explored many archetypes, but for our purpose we're interested in male and female archetypes alone.

Positive or neutral male archetypes

- Leader: This archetype embodies qualities of leadership, charisma, and responsibility. He inspires others, makes decisions for the greater good, and is often willing to sacrifice himself for his people or cause.

- Mentor/guide: This archetype is wise and experienced and serves as a source of guidance and wisdom. He helps with navigating challenges, learning important lessons, and growing as an individual.

- Protector: This archetype is characterized by a strong sense of duty and commitment to safeguarding others. He is courageous, loyal, and willing to put himself in harm's way to ensure the safety and well-being of those under his care.

- Sage/philosopher: This archetype embodies wisdom, introspection, and intellectual curiosity. He seeks truth and understanding, often through deep contemplation and study, and shares his insights with others to help them broaden their perspectives.

- Sage/wanderer: This archetype embodies a character who is on a journey of self-discovery, seeking knowledge, wisdom, and understanding. He is introspective, contemplative, and often detached from worldly attachments. The sage/wanderer may wander through different landscapes, both physical and metaphorical, encountering various challenges and experiences along the way. He seeks enlightenment and insight, drawing inspiration from nature, solitude, and encounters with others. The sage/wanderer archetype highlights the importance of introspection, curiosity, and the pursuit of truth in the journey of personal growth and transformation.

Positive or neutral female archetypes

1. Nurturer: This archetype is caring, compassionate, and deeply empathetic. She provides support, comfort, and encouragement to those around her, nurturing their emotional and physical well-being.

2. Heroine: Like the hero, this archetype embodies courage, resilience, and determination. She faces challenges head-on, overcomes adversity, and achieves her goals through her strength of character and resourcefulness.

3. Wise woman/mentor: Like the male counterpart, the wise woman archetype is a source of guidance and wisdom. She offers advice, perspective, and mentorship to others, drawing from her own life experiences and intuitive understanding.

4. Seeker/adventurer: This archetype is curious, adventurous, and open to new experiences. She embarks on journeys of self-discovery, exploration, and personal growth, seeking to expand her horizons and deepen her understanding of the world.

5. Reluctant survivor: This archetype embodies a character who has faced trauma or adversity and seeks safety and protection as a result. This character may be haunted by past experiences or struggles with feelings of vulnerability and fear. Despite their reluctance to confront danger, they possess resilience and inner strength that emerges when faced with adversity. The reluctant survivor may resist taking risks or venturing into unfamiliar territory, preferring the safety of familiar surroundings and the comfort of trusted allies. This archetype highlights the importance of healing and support for those who have endured hardship, while also showcasing the potential for growth and empowerment as they overcome their fears and reclaim their sense of security.

Some excellent work was done in the UK in the nineties to look at a series of values and how men and women had different affinities for them.[21] There is an extensive list here organized in a radar plot for ease of contrast. Trained AI was then used to determine how, in the public domain over the last decade, these values have featured for each gender.[22]

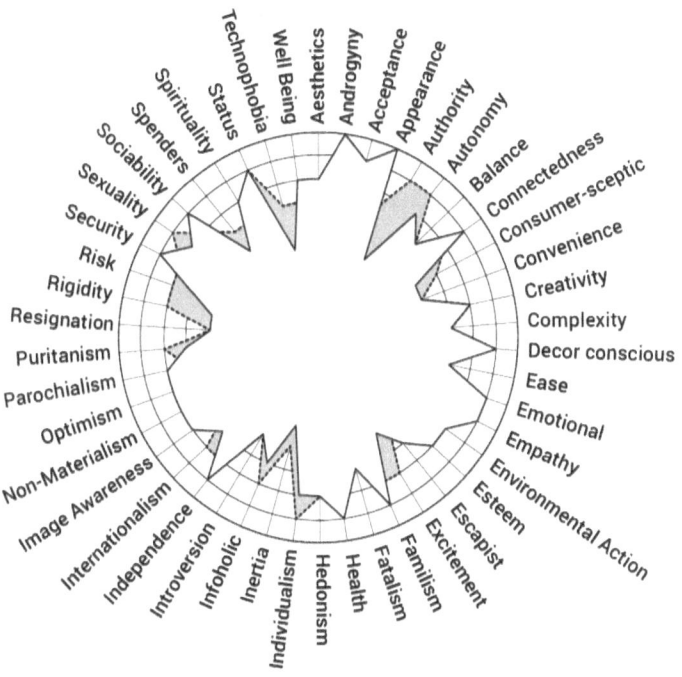

Figure 3: Values affinity: masculine and feminine archetypes

Revelation 1: Leadership behaviors

While in the early years of my professional career, one morning a friend stopped by my office. She was going to a luncheon where a Harvard School of Business study on gender and diversity was going to be presented, and she wanted me to join her. There was no such thing as inclusion and diversity committees in those years; it was a try-to-figure-it-out-by-yourself era.

I didn't know what awaited me. I'd been head down focusing on building my craft, exposing myself to field operations to gain hands-on knowledge, and being naïve in my bubble that I could be like my male counterparts and succeed. Although I can't trace the Harvard study presented that day, I came across almost verbatim, the takeaway from that luncheon in the book *The Developmental Social Psychology of Gender* which made a reference to the early research by the social psychologist Linda L. Carli, 1991.

How do males and females differ in their communication styles? Although the literature is quite extensive and the findings are somewhat mixed, when gender differences are reported, they generally reveal more competition, assertiveness, and authority by male speakers and more collaboration, agreeableness, and warmth by females.[23]

What was demonstrated to us with supporting statistics on that day was that, as an aspiring female leader, if you emulated your male counterparts' leadership styles, it would most likely backfire on you. I was at the centre of a male-dominated business and the key leaders I was surrounded with, especially at the C-suite level, were almost entirely men. Where would I find my inspiration? How could I authentically tap into the women's feminine winning leadership traits of warmth and competence, when it was so rarely observed in action?

My efforts to learn as much as I could and connect with all areas of my work, from mathematical models to field operations applied knowledge, were putting me on the right track. But trying to assert myself and compete as a leader to climb the corporate ladder in the same way as my role models would most likely backfire.

I had to double down on my warmth.

Often, I appeared to be very serious and driven at work. These traits were fine in the bubble of the company I worked for, but they wouldn't necessarily serve me well elsewhere. I resolutely started adopting a warm approach to my interactions; I tried it on for size and it soon became a habit and my strongest power—a power that would help me successfully navigate tough negotiations over multiple years on the international scene. For example, I was able to negotiate work programs and budgets with the local government over multiple cycles, while my predecessor, a smart and remarkably nice gentleman, had challenges because of his assertive and competitive style in negotiations.

Proof that my competency and warmth approach worked came from an unexpected place when, a decade later, we were reviewing salary bands relative to age groups in a graph. The graph was intended to be sanitized by the human resources department before sharing with the leaders of the company. To my surprise, though, I could easily decipher that I was the youngest and was two levels higher than everybody else.

So, if you identify as a man, focus on positively embodying assertive and competitive leadership traits, such as encouraging your teams to win against their competition or in valiantly achieving specific goals. If, on the other hand, you identify as a woman, consider positively embodying leadership traits of competency and warmth, such as being informed, resourceful, or knowledgeable, as well as smiling and embracing the team members' growth.

You have to be authentic in how you embody these traits; nothing will make your efforts fall flatter than inauthentic leadership. To support your journey, I've extracted key ideas for each leadership behavior and added a segment on what to be aware of for each:

1. **Assertiveness**
   - Confidence: Assertive leaders confidently express their ideas and decisions, inspiring confidence in their team.
   - Decisiveness: They make quick and firm decisions, which help to drive projects forward without unnecessary delay.

- Clarity: Assertive leaders communicate clearly and directly, ensuring that everyone understands their expectations and objectives.
- Courage: They aren't afraid to tackle difficult conversations or confront challenges head-on, fostering a culture of openness and honesty.
- Shadow side of assertiveness - overbearingness: There's a risk of being too forceful or dominating, which can alienate team members and stifle collaboration.

2. **Competitiveness**
   - Drive: Competitive leaders are highly motivated to achieve goals and excel, inspiring their team to strive for excellence.
   - Innovation: They constantly seek new ways to improve processes and stay ahead of the competition, fostering a culture of innovation.
   - Accountability: Competitive leaders hold themselves and others accountable for results, ensuring that everyone is committed to achieving success.
   - Resilience: They remain determined and resilient in the face of setbacks or challenges, motivating the team to persevere.
   - Shadow side of competitiveness—tunnel vision: The focus on winning can sometimes

lead to overlooking important ethical considerations or neglecting long-term sustainability.

3. **Warmth**

- Empathy: Warm leaders demonstrate empathy and understanding towards their team members, building strong relationships based on trust and mutual respect.

- Supportiveness: They provide emotional support and encouragement, creating a positive work environment where individuals feel valued and appreciated.

- Approachability: Warm leaders are approachable and open to feedback, making it easier for team members to voice their concerns or ideas.

- Inclusiveness: They celebrate diversity and ensure that everyone feels included and heard, promoting a sense of belonging.

- Shadow side of warmth—over-indulgence: being too focused on maintaining harmony or avoiding conflict may hinder necessary decision-making or constructive criticism.

I've often noticed that when a woman leader is warm, supervisors don't always believe that she's able to make the sort of tough decisions senior leadership positions require. A recent mentee mentioned that her boss would tell her in performance reviews that she was "too nice". She didn't know what to do with that feedback. Her brain told her *If I'm not nice, I'll be described as nasty,* plus it wouldn't be her authentic self. We explored her ability to make tough decisions despite her naturally friendly behavior, and it didn't seem to be a problem for her. She was aware of the dilemma that came in maximizing value drivers based on organizational needs. My recommendation was to look for an opportunity to declare authentically to her audience (which should include her boss) that they shouldn't mistake *niceness* with a *lack of toughness*. This is something I had to do at one point, and verbally expressing it had a huge impact on how my co-workers and my supervisor saw me.

4. **Competence**

    - Expertise: Competent leaders possess deep knowledge and expertise in their field, earning the respect of their team. They're often relied on for advice.

    - Problem-solving skills: They are adept at analyzing complex problems and finding effective solutions, inspiring confidence in their ability to overcome challenges.

    - Adaptability: Competent leaders are flexible and adaptable, able to navigate change and uncertainty with ease.

- Vision: They have a clear vision for the future and can articulate a compelling direction for the team, guiding them towards success.

- Shadow side of competence—perfectionism: The pursuit of excellence may sometimes lead to unrealistic expectations or micromanagement, which can demotivate team members and hinder productivity.

I was once told by a personal coach that perfectionism is the worst of qualities. Many great articles have been published on the subject in *Psychology Today*, including "Escaping the Perfectionist Trap: 7 Signs and 7 Solutions" in which Nuala G. Walsh suggests that recalibrating what matters, automating tasks to avoid procrastination, and challenging all-or-nothing thinking are interesting solutions to contemplate for someone struggling with perfectionism, a trait that can become a performance dilemma.[24]

This first revelation, related to broad preferences in leadership behaviors, applies indiscriminately to gender. Simply said, women just as much as men, tend to prefer having warm and competent women leaders and assertive and competitive men leaders. Conclusively, whether you're a woman or a man being led, you will have a biased preference for a leader being congruent with their own archetypes. Being aware of this bias gives you the opportunity to find it in yourself to authentically embody the leadership traits attributable to your gender archetype.

Revelation 2: Cultivate polarity

The uncomfortable topic of archetypes is counter current to recent rhetoric attempting to bring neutrality in our world rather than tapping into our respective powers. The construct felt discriminatory to me at first, and it wasn't something I appreciated right away. As a humanist who truly and authentically believes in equal opportunity and in maximizing the benefits of everyone's contributions, I promise the discomfort is necessary. It's one of the missing links in our societal approach to date: we thought the focus needed to be on gender neutrality for an inclusive environment to flourish. I hypothesize that this isn't the case! We'll make more satisfying progress by supporting everyone and nurturing their authentic self. If embraced broadly, this key will unleash phenomenal societal power and enable a breakthrough ahead in the slow-moving plateauing phase when it comes to advancing equality.

Let me tell you a personal story that unfolded more than a decade ago—a story that truly transformed my life and to this day affects how I act at home every day. I came across this principle that I wish I'd understood from the get-go. My spouse and I had decided to fly with our young kids to Florida to attend a weeklong workshop called "Date with Destiny" delivered by

Tony Robbins and his team. We had the luxury of grandparents who were more than happy to have the kids to themselves for the long away-days that were planned.

My spouse and I had different goals in attending. While his was more personal health and growth, mine was very much career oriented. I wanted to lay out the plan for the next decade to bring me to "destiny OR destination"—retirement. I was already a successful leader in my field and wanted to ensure I had the best momentum possible over the next decade.

Date with Destiny had a lofty agenda for the six days and covered such things as values, mission and purpose, and how to gain your own power. Day 3 was about relationships. We didn't think too much of it at first. I remember thinking, *our life together is awesome, so that won't be the focus of my time here.*

Wow was I wrong.

Something was about to change! At the time, my spouse and I were relatively new together, and we made a phenomenal team. We'd bought our house together, had two kids, moved countries, and had great careers. All that in just over six years, so we were still in the honeymoon phase. I felt that we were in an excellent place (and so did he).

The first day went well of the workshop, though it was a bit of an emotional ride about personal growth exploring our failures and successes, our life vision and values.[25] The second day was about taking a tally of what we'd accomplished and looking at our vision for the future. It also went well.

The practice in this three-thousand-plus retreat was to split people into groups of ten or fifteen. Spouses were placed in separate groups, so you could think deeply about your personal journey free from external influences. We made it a habit to meet for coffee during breaks to check in and see how everything was going. The first two days were smooth, and we laughed and chatted during our coffee breaks. On the third day, the relationship day, after being introduced to the concept of polarity, I remember vividly walking towards my spouse in the hotel hallway. We were looking into each other's eyes as we approached, both in full awareness of what was needed—a whole lot of work on our relationship!

My profile differs in many respects from the female archetype: I studied mechanical engineering—see the graph below on specialty representation. For example, only 18% of the UK's total first-year undergraduates in engineering and tech are women, even though women represent 57% of all first-year undergraduates. I worked as a processing plant operator (6.5% of plant operators are women and 93.5% of plant operators are men)[26]; occupied senior technical leadership roles (32% of women in engineering and technical roles are "onlies", meaning they're often the 'only woman in the room'—and they're underrepresented in leadership roles); and I ultimately became a person in the participative decision-making (PDM) which has recently gained attention as a measure of gender inclusivity in the workplace.[27] Finally, I have a genuine interest for finance and the global economy and love to watch *BNN* (Bloomberg's audience is 67% male and 33% female).[28]

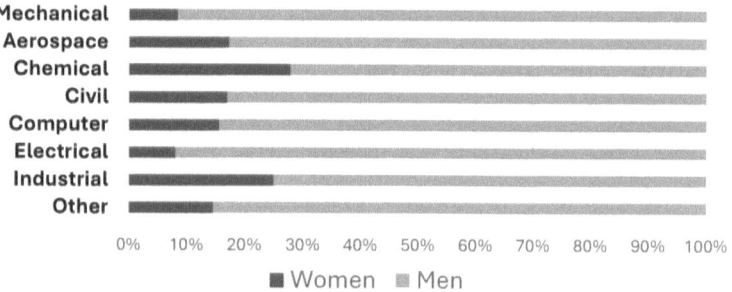

Figure 4: Representation of women in engineering[29]

That day, at Date with Destiny, we were introduced to a concept I had a hard time coming to terms with; that perhaps all these great qualities of being independent, autonomous, self-reliant, handy, and financially astute weren't serving me in my romantic relationship. In fact, these qualities were a momentous neutralizer of the chemistry and passion that fueled healthy and sustained romantic relationships. I've seen many women in my circle find excellent life partners, sometimes having kids with them, and ultimately feeling that the spark was eroded to the point where the relationship fell apart.

Sadly, before I became aware of this revelation, I was unable to help them meaningfully. In fact, I had a failed relationship myself behind me as well. This event made me think deeply about my life with my second spouse. While I was capable of doing many of the things that were traditionally carried out by the male in the relationship, when it came to my personal romantic life, I needed to let go to keep the passion and spark going. I needed to let go of aspects of our life I was good at such as finances and some of the security assurance in our life. The dilemma is that within the woman psychic archetype, there's a strong sense of needing security: security for our body, security for our emotions, security for our finances (this is often linked to the other two). The dilemma in this construct is that your partner has to be capable of taking on the challenge of being with what was once defined as a "challenging" woman.[30]

My dream in writing this book is that we all become extraordinary *challenging women*, capable of contributing fully to solve the most complex problems of our society—problems such as finding ways to send us to the moon, change the way we find our energies, develop the best artificial intelligence, produce outstanding mathematical models that reduce risks and maximize value, build mechanical and nano materials to deliver reliable alternatives to weakened body parts, AND at the same time become goddesses of our romantic lives.

For the readers identifying as male, this chapter is important in the context of helping your union to flourish long-term. Where there's a gap in knowledge and skills between you and your life partner, particularly in areas related to safety in the broader sense (whether psychological, physical, financial, or emotional), personal growth to bridge the gap is crucial. Such gaps might not be an issue at the beginning of the union, but over the years, enough insecurity will build that it could cause the end your relationship. The more independent a woman, the more skills are needed. The good news is that it can all be learned, and tackling these gaps will have a progressive and observable positive impact on your relationship's dynamic.

It's a dance—one where the woman in the romantic relationship needs to let go (and feel grounded and secure in doing so) and the man needs to embrace discovery and allow his ability to provide protection and reliability to grow.

As I was trying to come to terms with this construct, I was reminded of a presentation that reflected a situation very different from my own. I was in Indonesia when a highly educated scholarly woman made a presentation to expats about the cultural differences to observe and respect in the country. She was of Muslim faith, and at the time, I thought what she shared was greatly influenced by her religious practice. It probably was, yet beyond it all, what she was drawing on was this ancient brain chemistry dynamic. With our pursuit for equality, our global north cultures are moving away from nurturing this dance to the demise of many relationships which were initially, perfectly created polar attractions. She explained to us in the home women are behind their spouse, yet this does not keep them from being strong women in business (my champagne girlfriends will recognize themselves), thanks to the emancipation of women in the country, which is celebrated as Kartini day bolstered by a national holiday on April 21. Raden Adjeng Kartini was a nineteen century Javanese lady (*ibu* in Bahasa Indonesia). She was a feminist and an activist for the emancipation of women's rights in particular advocating for the importance of education for women and girls. While some recent publications have challenged the congruence between her messages and the recent associated festivities such as cooking competitions, fashion shows, etc. her letters published in the book *Darkness into Light*, represent her vision for empowerment and enlightenment of women in society.

I have been longing to make the acquaintance of a "modern girl" that proud, independent girl who has all my sympathy! She, who, happy and self-reliant, lightly and alertly steps on her way through life, full of enthusiasm and warm feeling; working not only for her own well-being and happiness, but for the greater good of humanity as a whole.[31]

I've tried to locate the name of the lady who presented this cultural training to us expatriates a few years back but couldn't. (*Ibu, if you read this book, I want to thank you for your open-hearted and vulnerable sharing that week.*) In a nutshell, she was conveying that while she was an educated career woman in her daily life, when she was at home, she was "behind" her spouse. It was a weird concept for me to grasp at the time as I feel and know I am equal to my life partner, but I was missing the point. Her point was she embraced her vulnerability, femininity, and embodies the "female" archetype in her home without feeling less empowered in her professional life.

There are other aspects of faiths I've never practiced that are elusive to me, and that's OK. By being open to our differences, we achieve great heights. I wish for this book to be neutral and build bridges in a sense that it mobilizes the human in us; regardless of faith, gender, or other associations. We'll make significantly more progress towards creating opportunities for everyone if we understand and share these nurturing polarity experiences. We are leaving many unions/partnerships/marriages in the dust by not nurturing this polarity, to the sadness of all involved (the partners themselves, the kids of the unions, and their extended families).

You might have heard the claim that half of all marriages end in divorce. I was curious where that statistic came from and found a United States study by Betsey Stevenson and Justin Wolfers (2007), "Marriage and divorce: Changes and their driving forces."[32] It appears to have once been true: 48% of American couples who married in the 1970s were divorced within 25 years. But since then, the divorce rate has fallen. It fell for couples married in the 1980s and again in the 1990s. The divorce rate has been falling, and the length of marriage has been increasing. And this trend has been observed in many other countries.

This is one of the pieces of great news of the last few decades and is perhaps attributable to increased flexibility and adaptability of society when it comes to unions; improved openness to delay marriages until partners have gotten to know themselves better (reduced societal pressure); and improved counsel and support when encountering marital challenges. In fact, more recent marriages seem to last longer and fewer end up in divorce. Hopefully, building awareness and sharing what's worked for us in our relationships will help this trend continue in a positive direction.

My journey on the path to embracing polarity continues. After leaving Date with Destiny, I started adopting easy techniques to get me into my feminine energy at the end of my workday: I change into soft clothes and put on relaxing or even dance music to make me move. I also focus on coming to my center and grounding my feet by walking barefoot, being in the present moment (rather than trying to solve my work problems in my head while gardening or attending my little one's baseball match). Meditation is great too.

More importantly, I started to explore how I could let go of some of the more "male" activities at home. It isn't that I don't roll up my sleeves to fix problems with HVAC (heating, ventilation, and air conditioning) or QC (quality control) check an investment position or two, but I leave it to my spouse to figure most of it out in his own way first. Sometimes it is as simple as letting him cover the bill at the restaurant while I enjoy sipping the rest of my drink. I also noticed my spouse doing things a little differently. He brings me flowers more often and enthusiastically plans getaways for us. I'll catch him walking on the outside of the curb, and doubling down on developing sophisticated strategies for our finances, which makes me feel secure, protected, and in good hands—a multitude of manly moves that don't go unnoticed by my animal brain.

Talking about the animal brain, the most primary activity a woman will do is carrying and giving birth to a baby. While I was pregnant with our second child, I had the gift of a lifetime when I ran into a senior leader at my work on my way to lunch. As she saw I was pregnant, she stopped and started to chat. She mentioned that she used hypnobirthing for both her children and highly recommended it. I bought the book *HypnoBirthing The Mongan Method: the natural ap-*

proach to safer, easier, more comfortable birthing.[33] It included a meditation CD that I listened to for six weeks prior to giving birth, and the tips the author gives in that book are transformative and unusual compared to current common practices. I remember how difficult it was to be in birthing mode at the hospital when I had my first child, as the nurses and hospital personnel were asking me a variety of questions and tapping into my left brain while I needed to be in my right brain to smoothly give birth. The advice given by Marie Mongan in her book was that while she advised getting clear as a couple of the various options and choices in your birthing plan, once in labor, your life partner needs to deal with all the logistics, inquiries, and decisions. In other words, you need to come into your feminine archetype to give birth; how fascinating!

As my polarity discovery continued, it was no coincidence that a few years later, I was matched with Brigitte Sumner as a coach—the author of the short and funny book *Give him back his balls*.[34] It's a go-to for a real reference on nurturing this polarity. Following her teachings, I evolved my femininity at home and so did my spouse his masculinity. Here's a quote from her book to give you a taste:

Men are solution oriented, give them a problem and they will solve it. In fact, they look for challenges and love them so much that they sometimes see them when they are not even there. They are competitive and want to win, which is evident in the way they gather status, material wealth and go about sports and other leisure pursuits.

They are compatible with Yang, fire, energy, sun, creation, heat, light, Heaven, and dominance.

Feminine energy is receiving, flowing, nurturing, lateral, emotional, all-seeing, caring, creating, gentle, compassionate and tidal. Women's moods can quickly swing from one extreme to another. Women are able to multitask, they can simultaneously chop vegetables, whilst overseeing homework and talk to a child's teacher on the telephone. A woman finds it hard to stay focused exclusively and not be distracted by what is going on around her. This allows her to be aware of more than one thing. Women are connection oriented, give them a problem and they'll talk about it. They are more about the team and giving everybody a fair chance, which is evident in the way they conduct their lives and interact with the world.

They are compatible with Yin, the moon, completion, cold, darkness, and material forms.

Masculine and feminine energies complement and attract each other like opposite poles on a magnet. We all have masculine and feminine energies and are all able to display parts of both.[35]

If you're in a relationship that's lost its spark, I highly encourage you to consider how you can authentically integrate AND appreciate your own gender compatibility. The ancient Chinese philosophy of yin and yang depicts this dance between the white and the black in entangled harmony. It's a fascinating symbol in how each side holds a bit of the other color (a black dot in the white and white dot in the black). It acts as a reminder that balance comes from living in one while honoring some of the traits (in a smaller quantity) of the opposite side.

In my relationship with my intimate partner, I try to strike a balance that resembles the yin/yang symbol—lots of black (passive, contemplative) energy and a little action and assertion in the places where I know I'm an ace. There are many sources which explore the essence of each duality but in summary they run along these lines:

Yin (feminine archetype)	Yang (masculine archetype)
Nature: Passive | receptive	Nature: Active | assertive
Feeling | Right brain activity	Thinking | Left brain activity
Spirit-centered consciousness	Ego-centered consciousness
A state of being	The act of doing
Heart	Mind
Flexibility	Rigid
Circle	Line
Soft | subtle energy	Hard | intense energy
Slow | steady movement	Fast | dynamic movement
Inward | descending direction	Outward | ascending direction
Night | moon	Day | sun
Calm | reflective emotion: Introspective	Excited | expressive emotion: Analytical
Yielding | adaptable approach	Forceful | direct approach
Listening | understanding communication	Speaking | persuading communication
Avoidant | compromising conflict style	Confrontational | competitive conflict style
Imaginative | intuitive creativity	Logical | practical creativity
Rest | recuperation in health	Exercise | activity in health
Cooperative | nurturing social behavior	Leading | organizing social behavior
Cautious | deliberate decision making	Decisive | quick decision making
Collaborative | supportive work style	Independent | ambitious work style

Historical archetype references across cultures

Other cultures have similar references:

Greek mythology

- **Masculine archetype: Zeus,** king of the gods, represents authority, power, and leadership. Known for his thunderbolt and ruling the sky.

- **Feminine archetype: Hera,** queen of the gods, represents marriage, motherhood, and family. Known as the goddess of women and marriage.

Hinduism

- **Masculine archetype: Shiva,** the destroyer and transformer, symbolizes strength, destruction of evil, and regeneration. Often depicted with a trident and a third eye.

- **Feminine archetype: Parvati,** the goddess of love, fertility, and devotion. Represents nurturing and creativity. Often depicted alongside Shiva, symbolizing balance and harmony.

Ancient Egypt

- **Masculine archetype: Osiris,** the god of the afterlife, resurrection, and agriculture. Represents regeneration and eternal life. Often depicted with green skin, symbolizing rebirth.

- **Feminine archetype: Isis,** the goddess of magic, motherhood, and fertility. Represents protection, healing, and nurturing. Known for her magical abilities and for resurrecting Osiris.

Norse mythology

- **Masculine archetype: Odin,** the chief of the gods, associated with wisdom, war, death, and poetry. Known for his quest for knowledge and his sacrifice of an eye for wisdom. He inspires personal growth and inner strength.

Feminine archetype: Freyja, goddess of love, beauty, fertility, and war. Represents both the nurturing and fierce aspects of femininity. Known for her chariot driven by cats and her role in selecting half of those who die in battle for her hall, Fólkvangr.

Chinese mythology:

- **Masculine archetype: Emperor Jade (Yu Huang)**, a supreme deity in Daoism, symbolizes order, authority, and justice. Often depicted as a wise and benevolent ruler.

- **Feminine archetype: Xi Wangmu (Queen Mother of the West)**, a goddess of immortality and prosperity who represents nurturing and life-giving aspects. Associated with the western paradise, the peach tree of immortality, stars, directions, and the sun and moon.

Christianity

- **Masculine archetype: God the Father** represents ultimate authority, creation, and paternal care. Often depicted as a wise, omnipotent, and omniscient being.

- **Feminine archetype: The Virgin Mary** represents purity, motherhood, and compassion. Venerated as the mother of Jesus Christ and a symbol of maternal devotion and grace.

Indigenous cultures

- **Masculine archetype: The Great Spirit (Wakan Tanka)** in the Lakota tradition. Represents creation, spirituality, and the interconnectedness and unifying force of all life. Often seen as a teacher, guide, and protector.

- **Feminine archetype: Pachamama** in Andean cultures. An Earth mother goddess who represents fertility, agriculture, and the nurturing aspect of nature. Revered as the provider of life and sustenance.

The importance here is what resonates for your authentic self in your own archetype and how you can think of embracing these states and behaviors positively in interacting with your life partner for the greater good of the relationship.

In many ways, we've been exposed to these two masculine and feminine archetypes almost every day since we were born, yet pausing and reflecting deeply on how these ancient learnings can be integrated into our personal romantic life is often something we overlook or simply don't even think about. Since my own deep reflection on this, I've shared it with a number of couples experiencing challenges and many ended up mending their way back to positive chemistry and enjoying the continuation of their unions together to the benefit of all involved: themselves, their children, their family, their friends.

It's important for me to share that on that journey of behaving in a way that is congruent with the female leadership archetype at work and at home congruent with my feminine essence, I don't always get it right. Often, I'll try something, and it will fall flat, but I have, and continue to make, great progress. What's beautiful is that the more I succeed, the better I feel overall and the happier and lighter my heart is, and that's what I wish for you, too.

Gender archetypes and expectations can be understood, accepted, and integrated into how our work and life personas evolve and dance together in our everyday life. The higher the intensity of responsibility in our work environment, the more conscious we need to be about the transitions between our work and personal lives. I'll cover some of my own and others' proven strategies to do so, yet just the awareness of the two distinctions is the foundational block to evolve your life in a way that works for you.

Chapter summary

Diversity and polarity

Introduces polarity as a means to unlock potential in diverse settings and emphasizes the importance of embracing authentic gender roles rather than pursuing gender neutrality. Suggests that societal progress in equity can be achieved by supporting individuals' authentic selves.

Revelation 1: Leadership behaviors

Archetypes are universal and innate models shaping human experience

Male archetypes	Female archetypes
In leadership	In leadership
Assertiveness	**Competence**
Positive - confidence | decisiveness;	Positive - expertise | problem-solving;
Shadow – overbearing.	Shadow - perfectionism.
Competitiveness	**Warmth**
Positive - drive | innovation;	Positive - empathy | supportive;
Shadow - tunnel vision.	Shadow - over-indulgence.

Revelation 2: Cultivate polarity

Archetypes are universal and innate models shaping human experience

Male archetypes	Female archetypes
In personal life	In personal life
Leader/Protector	**Nurturer/Heroine**
Duty and safeguarding others | Responsibility | Charisma	Support and compassion | Courage | Resilience
Sage/Philosopher	**Wise/Mentor**
Wisdom and understanding | Self-discovery journey	Guidance and experience. Growth journey

- **Impact on personal life**
  - Introduced to the concept of polarity and how in trying to advance equity and equality we might hinder romantic chemistry.
  - Realization that certain independent traits could neutralize passion in relationships.
  - Adjustments in personal behavior to balance masculine and feminine energies.
  - Notable improvements in romantic relationship dynamics after embracing these concepts.
- **Cultural insights**
  - Reference to Indonesian cultural practices and the celebration of Kartini Day, emphasizing women's education and empowerment.
  - An anecdote about a Muslim woman's balanced professional and personal life, respecting gender embodiment at home.
- **Broader implications**
  - Reflection on global divorce rates and how nurturing polarity might reduce relationship breakdowns.
  - Encouragement for both partners in a relationship to embrace and appreciate their gender archetypes for a balanced and fulfilling union.

- **Practical applications**
  - Practical techniques to transition from work to personal life and nurture feminine energy. Examples include changing attire, relaxing music, grounding exercises, and allowing the partner to take on certain responsibilities.
- **External references**
  - Mention of Brigitte Sumner's book *Give Him Back His Balls* for further exploration of gender polarity in relationships.
  - Summary of yin (feminine) and yang (masculine) characteristics from various cultural and philosophical perspectives.

Conclusion

Authentic embodiment of archetypal traits is key to effective leadership and is equally important in our personal lives. In history, we've seen many depictions and descriptions of feminine and masculine energies. While they serve as inspiration to channel our own power, it's essential we challenge our perspectives and are open to seeing anyone occupy any profession, no matter their gender. It's a societal imperative that we remove bias and barriers and enable everyone to be their whole self and encouraged to fully pursue their passions.

The importance of conscious transition between professional and personal roles to maintain harmony is also to be explored. Affirming there is a potential for more sustainability in unions with astute consideration of ancient wisdom and archetypes that resonate in a given situation.

In conclusion, understanding and authentically applying gender-specific traits can significantly and positively impact personal and professional development in diverse environments.

Chapter 3

Nurturing Equal Partnerships

Partnership is not a legal contract between two equal individuals. It's an emotional alliance between two people who are committed to each other's success.

Anonymous

How do we nurture the evolution of equal partnerships? Without the support you need at home, it's impossible—or only possible if you want to burnout, ramp-out, or simply give up in a few years down the road because the approach you chose simply isn't sustainable. Do you feel overwhelmed or that it's unmanageable to consider the career you loved because there isn't enough time in a day? It's a common feeling and one I hear frequently when someone asks for mentorship.

How can we share household responsibilities equally? How can we have each other's back at home and have our partners genuinely and positively feeling it? How can we set goals and make plans together as well as fuel a sentiment of belonging? And finally, how can we contribute toward each other's success?

Commitment 1: Sharing household responsibilities equally

It's disappointing that the last World Economic Forum Report of 2023 indicates things are getting worse, not better, for women's careers.[36] It makes us wonder about this conundrum of the "causality dilemma"— what needs to be fixed and improved first, household equality OR the advancement of women in their career.

Couples need to find equilibrium at home as a foundational block and create a world where the bias and disparity in home dividing duties are removed. This might seem counterintuitive at first because what makes sense financially might not align. The still lower salaries and benefits experienced by women around the world will impede and most likely influence the balance. In fact, a recent publication by Forbes Advisor, "Gender Pay Gap Statistics in 2024" highlights important trends when it comes to pay equity.[37] The publication uses a recent report by AAUW-empowering women since 1881 as a reference to describe that:

- Women earn 16% less than men on average—or women earn just 84 cents for every dollar a man makes. The controlled gender pay gap (which considers factors such as job title, experience, education, industry, job level and hours worked) is currently at 99 cents for every dollar men earn. In 1963, a woman made 59 cents for each dollar earned by a man; in 2010 that number had increased to 77 cents—an improvement of half-a-cent on average annually. The Center for American Progress projects that gender pay equity won't become a reality until 2056.[38]

- Despite the push for equal pay for equal work, women continue to earn less than men in nearly every occupation, from entry-level positions to the C-suite. The gender pay gap for entry-level positions is 18.4%, while even when controlling for job characteristics, women at the executive level still earn only 95 cents for every dollar earned by men, and in the uncontrolled group, the pay gap widens to 73 cents.

- A twenty-year-old woman just starting full time, all-year-round work stands to lose $407,760 over a forty-year career compared to her male counterpart.

So if you had two people on household duties and had to pick someone to bring little Abe to the dentist, who would you pick?

Parent A with a salary of X=$1.00 or Parent B with a salary of Y=$0.84?

Yet, if the enablement that comes from equally sharing duties at home doesn't happen, there's little hope for uplifting everyone to their full potential in their career. Just by virtue of pausing and intentionally moving towards evenly covering the week's appointments, family commitments, and other logistics in a balanced way, it will change the way you think and navigate day-to-day matters. My spouse and I had a few things we did which worked well, particularly if both spouses work outside the home. To manage the week's family related commitments, we would:

1. **Plan it:** Without discipline, you won't get there. The best way to remove bias is by applying a process that brings neutrality to the approach. Neutrality doesn't always mean that every week will be even, because you might be out of town, you might have a stiff deadline, or you might be the incident command on an emergency. Every Sunday we looked at the calendar for the next two weeks and determined who was on tap for what.

2. **Plan contingency**: No matter where you live, you won't be able to do it alone. Find the courage to show vulnerability and ask for help—a retired neighbor, a long-time friend, a parent from your kid's school or their teenage children, and if you're lucky enough to have family in your

city/household, your family members. Knowing who's in town that week and who could help at a moment's notice is crucial because if something comes up last minute you know where to go. In a worst-case scenario, hire a nanny, an Uber/Lyft driver, or someone from other support services in your area.

3. **Share it:** As my role always came with an assistant, we communicated our plans with them so they could integrate our look ahead in my work schedule. This was also important because if you're in the middle of a negotiation and it runs late, you can't leave your daughter waiting on the curb—and there's no better way to leave money on the table during a negotiation than when you don't give it all your attention.

4. **Consider remote working:** With the evolution of media platforms, increased reliability of networks and tools for remote meetings and conversations, consider taking such things as parent/teacher interviews remotely. Also consider if business meetings are required in person every time, or can you take the odd one by staying home instead of jumping on a plane?

Innovative options are arising around the world to support this division of tasks: Spain hopes their domestic tasks application will ensure men pull their weight. The free app launched in 2023 is designed to shed light on the 'mental load' overwhelmingly carried by women when it comes to chores.[39] There are also books such as Kate Mangino's *Equal Partners—Improving Gender Equality at Home*.[40] Mangino interviewed a diverse group of forty equal men partners who do half of the physical and cognitive household labor. She says setting out expectations at the beginning of a relationship is:

Hugely important ... it's much easier to establish patterns from the beginning than to change a relationship 10 or 20 years into it. I think being clear about expectations, and holding each other accountable from the start, is critical.[41]

That household-chores-and-family-commitments dance is evolving. While my mom worked as my parents were raising us, they were of a more traditional generation. My mom had significant expectations for how the house needed to look and she coached us, in the nicest way imaginable, to do chores exactly as she wanted them done. She was (and still is) so nice and considerate that we couldn't say no. In fact, she was so convincing that eventually we cleaned the house out on our own accord to her standards—talk about leadership! She trained us well, showing by example, being consistent, and celebrating together once the chores were complete, i.e. we'd bake together, play cribbage or Scrabble.

In retrospect, I wish my dad had given me as much guidance and nurturing of my skills in the garage as he's a gifted woodworker and fixes everything intuitively based on years of experience, and sometimes much trial and error.

My parents achieved balance in their own way, with the lens they were using to look at the world. At one point, though, my mom shared she felt she was lifting more than her share with a full-time job. Why was she always on tap to decide what we were going to have for dinner or in charge of noticing that laundry was overdue? The reality is, her standards were high to the detriment of other things she could have pursued, and my dad, while doing little cooking or laundry, did a lot in the garage and around the house—shoveling snow, raking and cutting the grass, building furniture to help with affordability of goods we needed and thus significantly improving our quality of life. My mom's dedication to healthy meals, homework, and a clean and beautiful home also significantly improved our quality of life.

We need to align on our priorities at home first, then decide how we'll divvy up tasks and challenge that gender-typical allocation so our daughters become as handy as our sons in the wood shop and our sons are just as good at knowing how to split the laundry into appropriate piles and cook a great meal.

With the vision that we achieve the dream of more and more women (and men) continuing to pursue the career they love, ultimately this will translate into more and more collective wealth and dual-income households adapted societal environments. With improved household wealth, farming out the chores nobody in the household wants to do to a professional (or finding technology to do the work) will become more possible, save relationships, and help advance our collective productivity index.

Commitment 2: Collaborative design thinking in relationships

Design thinking in relationships is a key to success. It's one of my favorite mind-constructs and a concept I use at virtually every leadership or decision-making table I touch. I had the privilege of visiting the Sanford Engineering Life Design Lab and was exposed to the idea that through removing the shackles in the design-thinking vernacular called "dysfunctional beliefs" and by focusing on what we want to create, we're generally much happier with the solution to a problem. Happier because the solution meets more of our conscious and unconscious desires, values, and criteria. Design thinking is a mindset and approach to problem-solving and innovation anchored around human-centered design. While it can be traced back centuries (perhaps even longer), it gained traction in the modern business world after Tim Brown, CEO and president of design company IDEO, published an article about it in the *Harvard Business Review*.[42]

Design thinking is different from other innovation and ideation processes in that it's solution-based and user-centric rather than problem-based. This means it focuses on the solution to a problem instead of the problem itself.[43]

Collaborative design thinking is therefore to come together to arrive at a common vision—to visualize and ultimately create the life we want.

Setting goals and making plans together

To use a marine analogy, coming together to share where we want to take the ship, what transit path we'll use to get there, what are the risks in the journey and how we will ensure we have mitigations along the way can significantly improve our odds of getting to destination. It seems intuitive that setting goals and making plans together is at the heart of relationship success, yet few take the time to design-think.

There are three spectrums to help organize your thoughts and approach, and all three are necessary to achieve long-term success. This frame came to me when I was responsible for leading an integrated—planning team and realized we were excellent in the first thirty days of our plans, and decent with our long-term strategic plan, but we fell short when it came to the near term and opportunistic department.

The distinct spectrums are systematic long, systematic short, and opportunistic near.

Systematic long—the most inspirational spectrum:

Commonly referred to as *long range planning*, it's often eighteen months out and more. In the context of work, it would be your work program and budget (WP&B) for the following year along with your plans for the remaining life of the asset.

In our personal lives, it means planning with the long game in mind—the next chapter, retirement, or ultimate life goal. I use it in meditation to imagine the world I aspire to create and help me prioritize systematic short and opportunistic near goals.

I call it *systematic long* because the cycle naturally emerges annually: January to January, September to September, my birthday to my birthday. And it usually brings inspiration to reach beyond and dream a little. It's a reflective time which also commonly involves taking a tally of how far you've come, and as a result it has a grounding effect.

Systematic short—the "stay the course if possible" spectrum:

This is your weekly, bi-weekly, 30-day or 90-day plan. In this spectrum, the ship has, or will have soon, left the dock and is on its way. Significant resources have been allocated, and while it's not impossible to change your mind about something, it will come at a cost or be difficult to optimize because of a lack of time between the decision to pursue and the execution time. In some cases, you might need to bring in an emergency response team to deal with a crisis that derails the 90-day plan ahead.

In our personal lives, it's akin to: we've planned the extra-curricular activities, booked the travel, and are doing the two-week look ahead mentioned earlier to ensure we have the resources we need to smoothly carry out the plans.

My best life analogy for this spectrum is my grandfather. He was the finest driver I knew. He used defensive driving while behind the wheel but also excelled at journey management, confirming our needs well in advance as to when and where we wanted to go, ensured he had the right transport means, and was always reliable. Riding with him was the smoothest of experiences because he never hurried, and he was attentive, calm and stayed the course.

Opportunistic near—the optimize and innovate spectrum:

So much money and so many opportunities are missed by underestimating the superpower of the three-to-eighteen-month spectrum. This is the space where you can afford to use broad "unshackled" ideas to optimize, improve, upgrade, and refine resources appropriately, and adjust without creating a crisis. The dilemma is often that this is rarely an area of focus. This spectrum is the period where you can be the most strategic because you have enough knowledge about your environment, the variables at play (in general narrowing of uncertainty ranges) AND have enough time to make a difference without causing a derailer (an event that causes the plan to go off track), incurring significant costs, or creating a crisis. There are few exceptions such as in the case of mega projects where changes could cause a derailer, but for most of our life events, the risk of creating issues is low. This is the spectrum where opportunities will arise, and the odds of being able to take advantage of them are excellent.

In our personal lives, it means taking the time to reflect together (we like doing it as a family), plan and optimize the near-term passions we like to pursue, the opportunities we don't want to miss (like your favorite band's upcoming concert), the university spot you'd like to secure, the wedding you'd like to plan, the book you'd like to write, etc. It's a time to bring out all the notes you've jotted down for the "wouldn't it be great if" category, and to take a little time for research and to nurture the connections you need to advance your vision. This is a fantastic and invigorating planning spectrum, one I recommend doing with positive, energizing, and supportive people.

Psychological safety plays a significant role as well. Since the term was coined by Harvard Business School professor Amy Edmondson in 1999, the benefits of psychological safety in the workplace have been well established.[44]

According to an article by McKinsey & Company, psychological safety means feeling safe to take interpersonal risks, to speak up, to disagree openly, to surface concerns without fear of negative repercussions or pressure to sugarcoat bad news.[45] Psychological safety nurtures an environment where people feel encouraged to share creative ideas without fear of personal judgment or stepping on toes. In this kind of environment, it feels safe to share feedback with others, including negative upward feedback to leaders about where improvements or changes are needed. It's OK to admit mistakes, be vulnerable, and speak truth to power. When psychological safety is present in the workplace or at home, it creates a more innovative, stronger community.

By collaboratively design-thinking your relationships using both a systematic AND opportunistic approach, the resilience, as well as the understanding and trust you'll build together will enhance and nurture equal partnerships. This integrated planning tip is one of the most powerful to remove barriers and fall into alignment with our shared purpose. More importantly, it makes you feel a full-fledged contributor to the success you achieve together, solidifies your allyship (or allies), knowing the elements are coming together nicely in support of that shared vision. This is particularly important when things become more challenging, and break-ins (disturbances, intrusions, hiccups) come your way; because they will.

Chapter summary

The chapter builds on previous discussions about economic opportunities through embracing diversity and the influence of gender archetypes. The focus shifts to nurturing equal partnerships both at home and work to create sustainable success.

Key points

Importance of equal partnerships

- True partnership starts at home, and without support there, professional aspirations can suffer due to burnout or overwhelming responsibilities.

- Sharing household responsibilities equally is crucial for both partners to achieve their full potential in their careers.

Sharing household responsibilities equally

- Statistics indicate a persistent gender pay gap, with women earning less than men in nearly every occupation.

- The financial rationale often leads to women taking on more household duties, which hampers their career advancement.

- Equal division of household tasks can change perspectives and support both partners' professional growth.

Strategies for equitable household management

1. **Plan it:** Regularly review and plan family commitments and household duties together.

2. **Plan contingency:** Have a backup support system in place for unforeseen circumstances.

3. **Share it:** Communicate plans with assistants or others involved to seamlessly integrate family and work schedules.

4. **Consider remote options:** Use technology to manage some responsibilities remotely where possible.

Innovative support solutions

- Emerging technologies and applications, like Spain's domestic tasks app, help us to highlight and share the mental load of chores.

- Books like Kate Mangino's *Equal Partners* provide insights and strategies for improving gender equality at home.

Collaborative design-thinking in relationships

- **Setting goals and making plans together:** Use collaborative design thinking to set a shared vision and plan for the future.

Three spectrums of planning for success

- **Systematic long-term:** Plan for long-range goals and life aspirations.

- **Systematic short-term:** Focus on immediate plans and commitments, ensuring resources are allocated efficiently. This spectrum includes the short-term tactical management of the day-to-day tasks and immediate needs, ensuring flexibility and responsiveness.

- **Opportunistic near-term:** Use this period (3 to 18 months) to optimize and innovate without causing disruption. This is a spectrum teeming with potential, yet for which intentional planning is often neglected.

Conclusion

Equal partnerships at home and work enhance resilience, trust, and mutual support, enabling both partners to achieve their professional and personal goals.

By integrating systematic and opportunistic approaches, couples can design a fulfilling and balanced life together, overcoming challenges and building a shared vision for the future.

Chapter 4

Embracing and Enabling Diversity in Business and at Home

When you believe you know the truth, it is better that you know you believe than to believe that you know.

Jacques Languirand[46]

Creating inclusive environment cultures

A behind the wheel pondering: why do we see more men driving than women? I find it keeps me in my feminine archetype when we're rushing to a date night; I favor having my spouse drive us. I also find it intimidating maneuvering a car in old European towns' tight and steeply sloped parking lots when driving the large car we've rented to transport the entire family plus luggage. Somehow, my spouse has much higher risk tolerance than me and he doesn't seem to be as fazed by it.

Research indicates that several factors contribute toward the higher prevalence of men driving cars compared to women.

Cultural and social norms: Car ownership and driving are often associated with masculinity and independence. Historically, men have been more likely to be the primary drivers in households, influenced by societal expectations and gender roles. This cultural connection between cars and male identity persists, with car ownership symbolizing material wealth and social status for men more than for women.[47]

Travel patterns and responsibilities: Studies show that while men and women make a similar number of daily trips, men tend to drive longer distances and prefer using cars. In contrast, women's trips often involve multiple stops for family, work, and social responsibilities, leading them to opt for public transport, walking, or cycling when available. This difference in travel behavior influences the frequency and necessity of car use.[48]

Road safety perceptions and infrastructure: Women are generally more concerned about road safety and tend to choose safer and more sustainable modes of transport if they feel secure. However, transport systems and urban planning have traditionally been designed with male car drivers in mind, often neglecting the safety and convenience needs of women. This can deter women from driving and push them toward other forms of transportation.[49]

Risky driving behavior: Men are statistically more likely to engage in risky driving behaviors such as speeding, driving under the influence, and aggressive driving. These behaviors result in a higher number of fatal accidents involving male drivers, despite women being more likely to get into minor accidents. The perception of these risks may discourage women from driving.[50]

Policy and infrastructure changes: Some cities are starting to address disparities by redesigning urban spaces to be more inclusive of non-driving modes of transport and targeting campaigns to encourage men to adopt sustainable mobility options. These efforts highlight the need to understand and address gender-specific mobility patterns to reduce car dependency among men and improve overall transport safety and sustainability.[51]

Understanding these factors is crucial for developing policies and for urban designs that promote equitable and sustainable transportation for all genders. But when it comes to the statistics, women have been proved to be overall better drivers for our societal good. They just happen not to take the lead due to other factors.

A recent publication by Jason L Arthur highlights fascinating statistics on the subject.[52]

- Statistically, women are safer drivers than men.
- In 2020, 75% of fatal crashes involved male drivers.
- Women drivers have a higher fatality rate in serious accidents than men.
- For every 100 million miles traveled, men have a crash rate of 2.1, while women have a crash rate of 1.3, meaning that men are 61% more likely to get into an accident than women.
- Of a sample of just over 9 million drivers involved in road traffic accidents in 2020, 41% were female and 59% male.
- More than three times as many male drivers were involved in fatal car crashes in 2020 compared to female drivers.
- Based on 2017–2020 data, men accounted for 73% of all traffic violations and 75% of speeding offenses.
- 58% of drivers involved in non-fatal injury car crashes in 2020 were male, and 42% were female.
- 47% more male drivers were involved in property-only crashes in 2020 than female drivers.
- 22% of male drivers in fatal crashes in 2020 had a blood alcohol concentration (BAC) of at least 0.8.

In contrast, only 16% of female motorists in fatal crashes drove with a BAC of at least 0.8.

- Taking into account all accident types (fatal, injury only, and property damage only), the highest driver involvement rate is amongst male drivers aged 16-20 years.

- A 2019 survey revealed that men (32.9%) were more likely to have fallen asleep at the wheel compared to women (22.2%).

Although the number of licensed drivers in 2021 was split almost equally between men (115.2 million) and women (117.6), women buy 62% of all new cars sold in the U.S. and influence more than 85% of all car purchases. These are all United States figures, but we could all benefit from improving our urban designs to entice more women to take the wheel, and we might in turn benefit as a society. However, at the end of the day, it is what works well for us in our environmental circumstances and what drives us; pun intended.

What can we do? We could follow the examples of cities that have adopted specific measures, such as Vienna, Austria, which has been a pioneer in gender-sensitive urban planning, incorporating women's needs into its public transport system and urban design since the 1990s.[53]

Here are a few potential avenues to explore:

- **Enhanced street lighting:** Ensure all streets, parking areas, and pathways are well lit to improve safety and visibility, reducing the risk of crime and increasing comfort for women driving at night.

- **Secure parking facilities:** Design secure, monitored parking garages with controlled access and surveillance cameras. Provide designated parking spaces for women in well-lit, high-traffic areas closer to entrances.

- **Improved signage and wayfinding:** Install clear, easily readable signage for navigation, parking, and pedestrian crossings to reduce stress and enhance the driving experience for all.

- **Safe pedestrian pathways:** Develop wide, well-maintained, and well-lit pedestrian pathways to encourage walking and ensure safety when transitioning from parking areas to destinations.

- **Protected bike lanes:** Implement protected bike lanes to provide safe alternatives to driving, as women are more likely to cycle when a safe infrastructure is available.

- **Family-friendly infrastructure:** Create family-friendly infrastructure such as drop-off zones near schools and childcare centers, making it easier to juggle multiple responsibilities when navigate urban environments.

- **Accessible public transport hubs:** Design multimodal transport hubs that integrate parking with public transport options, facilitating easy transitions between driving and public transport.

- **Mixed-use development:** Plan for mixed-use neighborhoods that combine residential, commercial, and recreational spaces, reducing the need for long car journeys and making daily errands more convenient.

- **Traffic calming measures:** Implement traffic calming measures such as speed bumps, roundabouts, and pedestrian crossings to enhance safety and reduce aggressive driving behaviors that can deter women from driving.

- **Participatory planning and gender-sensitive policies:** Involve women in the urban planning process to gather their insights and address their specific needs. Develop and implement policies that ensure transport and urban design budgets consider gender-specific requirements.[54]

By incorporating these improvements, urban developers can create environments that are safer, more accessible, and more inviting for women drivers, ultimately contributing to a more equitable urban experience for all residents. Our cars are evolving to require less and less of our intervention and participation and in due course will become more neutral to both genders.

Inclusive environments—THE right tools

Besides driving, I thought of other examples where my brain had (without doing any research) assumed that female traits might be less adapted to specific leadership roles—for example, being an incident command in an emergency situation. This is a role I've held many times over the years, and it requires a leadership style that's more command-and-control, because of the lack of time for bringing people along through the empathetic and more indirect approaches often associated with successful female leadership traits.

Studies such as "Women are Better Leaders During a Crisis" by Jack Zenger and Joseph Folkman show that my assumptions aren't quite accurate in that case either.[55] There is a variety of notions rooted in assumptions yet, when we take a deeper look, we realize these notions are more the effect than the cause. As we investigate the root causes of why it is that way, we often find these assumptions are revealed to us as just that: assumptions.

Many aspects of our world seem to be male dominated, but when we scratch the surface of skills, efficiencies, and rationale for why they are, we often fall short of finding a meaningful explanation. We quickly understand it's because women must often adapt to the point they might never be as comfortable as men in the environment. If they were provided with improved design and a suitable infrastructure, they might thrive. As a minimum, it might help them avoid abandoning the activity or task all together. The insidious load of sustained adaptations, in a given environment, should not be underestimated. While not significant at the beginning, these adaptations become significant over time. This is often not because of a lack of ability to learn, knowledge, or even skills. It's simply that the environment has not been designed for them in mind and their specific needs aren't met.

This brings me to a personal story. I was hiking with a great friend of mine, Tracey, who's currently a senior supply chain executive managing an international portfolio. When she started working, because of her petite build, no personal protective equipment (PPE) coveralls fitted her. She decided she'd had enough and phoned the suppliers, insisting they start a line for women's bodies—including pregnant women. Thanks to Tracey, many of us no longer have to adapt to poorly fitting coveralls and other PPE. And since then, we've seen more and more offerings of that nature. But even to this day, you need to look for them.

We also now have easier-to-handle tools, forklifts, etc. While women will continue to be on average physically weaker than men given average size differences and the physiological circumstances of our bodies, the differences aren't that significant in the grand scheme of things. Really when you look at the world, there's a threshold of weight that can be lifted by a man and beyond that, what do we do? We get machinery to help. Because we've been in a male-dominated environment (especially in operations and STEM), our world is adapted to the male threshold. We just need to adapt our infrastructure to the female threshold in areas where men dominate and adapt to the men's threshold in areas where women dominate, to remove barriers inhibiting access.

I love my tools, and I have a doctor's briefcase-like tool kit at home filled with tools adapted for me. I also have big tools to give me more leverage, such as a long iron pipe for my box wrench, a crowbar, and a variety of high friction non-slip options to maximize my grip. On my first mechanical job as a plant operator, I had to transport a pipe-wrench using a wheelbarrow because I was unable to swing a big valve by myself. The guys on the team could have helped, but they well knew I had to learn how to manage and be capable of doing it on my own—and I did! I still remember that day, smiling at my team leader watching from the control room and smiling back at me in support as I walked across the window with the big wrench in a wheelbarrow.

I succeeded on that day: first I swung the valve myself and second, I knew I was respected and supported psychologically by my teammates. We laughed together about the situation at lunchtime, which made me feel even more part of the team. Nowadays, there's much more automation to swing large valves like the one I had to deal with, and this is the world we are ready to move into to give opportunity for everyone. In other areas, I see adaptations such as access to gender neutral toilets and the recent emergence of the pink porta-potties on worksites. Every time we drive by one, I make a point of underscoring to my daughter that women work there.

Human factors in design is a broad and sophisticated subject. It's also far-reaching, but let's conclude this section by acknowledging that much can be done to adapt our world to make it more possible for all to consider pursuing any passion, any career, no matter their birth gender.

Training on inclusion and diversity

What's resonated in one of the organizations I worked with, and what seems to be supported in the work environment, is that inclusion has to come first, and then progress towards diversity has a higher chance of being sustained. In the past few decades, emphasis was put on hiring diversity. Ah, these long conversations about hiring targets! It turns out if your environment isn't inclusive, such efforts will fall flat and be elusive as they won't allow for long-term retention of the diversity hired. Some of them will decide to go on their own or you'll let them go because they don't fit in, they don't speak the same language as you, they don't see the world in the way you do, or they even sometimes get mad and become "challenging women" or "challenging men" as referenced by Su Maddock in her book *Challenging Women- gender, culture and organization.*[56]

They might become challenging because they're not supported, or worse they're harassed and subject to micro aggressions from the get-go. Ultimately, because they're trying to adapt to an unfavorable environment, they might become more irritable than the person next door.

As a part of the Society of Decision Professionals, I once jointly presented a panel on bias. We all contributed a piece and Laura my co-presenter had a very interesting interactive exercise for us called the *circle of trust*. It went somewhat like this:

1. Write down the names of five to ten of your go-to people (not including your family). Think of them as your inner circle—people you consider trustworthy and whose advice you seek when making decisions.

2. For all the categories below, put a tick next to the people on your list who share the same trait as you for that category.

    – gender

- sexual orientation
- race/ethnicity
- age
- education level
- nationality
- ableness
- native language

Her segment was about affinity bias: the tendency for individuals to gravitate toward and show preference for people who share similar characteristics, backgrounds, or interests. Becoming authentically aware of that tendency is the first step in training yourself to explore others who might not fit that go-to profile. I consider myself open-minded and non-discriminating, yet my circle was way, way narrower than I dared admit.

Training on inclusion needs to start with awareness. Ultimately, it should also be hands on where we're put in situations, whether that's solving a problem together, helping the community together, playing games together—in other words, we should build psychological bridges together.

The most effective strategies are:

- **Interactive and engaging formats**: Training that involves active participation, such as workshops, role-playing, and group discussions tends to be more effective than passive formats like lectures or videos.

- **Customized content**: Tailoring the training to the specific context and needs of the organization and its employees can enhance its relevance and impact.

- **Ongoing efforts**: Training should not be a onetime event but part of a continuous commitment to inclusion and diversity (I&D). This can include follow-up sessions, ongoing education, and integration into everyday business practices.

- **Top-down and bottom-up approaches**: Support from leadership is crucial. When leaders actively participate and demonstrate a commitment to I&D, it can foster a more inclusive culture. Additionally, encouraging grassroots initiatives and employee resource groups can also be effective.

- **Focus on implicit bias**: Training that addresses biases related to unconscious attitudes, stereotypes, or associations that influence our understanding, actions, and decisions without our awareness. and provides strategies for recognizing and mitigating them can be particularly impactful.

- **Measurement and accountability**: Implementing mechanisms to measure the effectiveness of I&D

initiatives and holding individuals and the organization accountable for progress can help ensure that training leads to tangible outcomes.

Subjects to consider

- **Understanding diversity and inclusion**: Basic concepts, the importance of I&D, and the benefits of a diverse and inclusive workplace.

- **Implicit bias**: What implicit biases are, how they form, and strategies to mitigate their impact.

- **Cultural competence**: Understanding and respecting cultural differences and improving cross-cultural communication.

- **Inclusive leadership**: Training leaders on how to foster an inclusive environment and lead diverse teams effectively.

- **Conflict resolution**: Strategies for addressing and resolving conflicts that may arise from diversity-related issues.

- **Bystander intervention**: Teaching employees how to recognize and intervene in discriminatory or exclusive behaviors.

Bias in the workplace

There are so many types of bias that it's nearly impossible to tackle them all, let alone all at once. There are two main categories: conscious bias (tip of the iceberg) and unconscious bias (the part of the iceberg we don't see). Some of the most common are cognitive biases, and research suggests there are more than 175 different types. They all refer to deviation from standards of judgment whereby you may create inferences, assessments or perceptions that are unreasonable. You may also recollect past experiences incorrectly. These perceptions may dictate a person's behavior or attitude in a positive or negative way.[57]

The fact they're unintentional and insidious as they influence our choices is a problem when it comes to advancing and paving the way for everyone to reach their full potential. Like most people, I think of myself as open-minded and fair. However, a relatively recent event made me realize a cognitive bias that left me speechless.

One of the engineering directors on my team came to me with a woman's resume that had been dropped off by our EVP for an engineering role posted for his team. The request to me was, "Do we have to consider this latest entry? We're fairly far along in the recruitment process."

I answered, "Not necessarily if this latest entry doesn't compete when compared with the candidates already retained for the upcoming interviews."

- "You see, we've received nearly two hundred applicants for this role," he said, "and human resources selected the top thirty resumes. Out of which, a senior person on my team and I reviewed and invited three candidates for an interview."

- "Out of curiosity, how many out of the three candidates invited are women?"

- "None."

- "How about we go back to the top thirty and select the top woman candidate?" I suggested. "Then you can compare that top woman's resume with the senior woman's resume from our EVP."

- Ultimately, we agreed that one additional candidate, a woman, would be added to the roster of interviewees i.e. four candidates (three men and one woman). I was happy with that ratio as the sought after candidate had to have more than fifteen years of experience and the ratio of the graduates in those years was less than one in five.

- Fast forward, the woman invited to the interview along with three men, ultimately didn't get the role. I still felt good that I'd positively influenced the leader to consider candidates in the ratios close to gender availability for the total candidate pool until about two months later when I was in the office of a senior and very competent human resource leader. I told her the story as a good example of trying to advance towards gender equity. Her comment was, "Josee, you know she had zero chance of getting the job?" I said no, she had one in four (25%) chance of getting the job.

She sent me home to watch a short explanatory video on the subject called Why So Few 'Diversity Candidates Are Hired – Harvard Business Publishing and indeed, due to our ancient brain cognitive bias, we subconsciously don't like the element that's different to all the others. Why? It makes it harder for our minds to deal with the difference.[58] As a result, the different element won't be selected almost every time because our brain is busy trying to compare the other three. This was illustrated in research conducted at the University of Colorado just over ten years ago![59] It's by pure luck that women in STEM find a job at all!

Composition of finalist pools vs. likelihood of hiring a woman
Source Stefanie K. Johnston et al HBR.org
(Study based on a pool of 598 finalists for university teaching positions)

👩 👩 👩 👨 = 67%
👩 👩 👨 👨 = 50%
👩 👨 👨 👨 = 0%

Every time I succeeded at getting hired, I was in competition with at least one other woman. This had the effect of neutralizing this simplification bias by offering a choice between two or more entities of similar nature. When there's a pool of candidates and I'm in the final stage of the interview, I always ask for the profiles of the other candidates and, now knowing about this bias, you should too. This bias holds also true if you're the only person of color or the only man.

Another interesting bias was recently highlighted in the political sphere where women are in tough competitions with men counterparts, such as in presidential races. Studies show individuals are twice as likely to refer to a man in power by their last name versus a woman. Powerful women are called by their first name.[60] This is a subtle and impactful nuance that affects judgment of eminence and competence: think Einstein, Shakespeare, Lincoln. Gender equality will continue to be illusive without systematically and intentionally unpacking and addressing these insidious behaviours and norms.

Here are some tips and tricks to neutralize some biases:

Workaround groupthink: Groupthink can be reduced by having group members play the contrarian or bringing in a trained facilitator in important discussions.

Leaders should hold off judgment: If you're leading a group, think hard about when to endorse an option. Waiting until all the facts and viewpoints are in can reduce self-serving biases, groupthink, and overconfidence.

Ensure a fair table: Change the mix of your sample by ensuring there is no one entity fundamentally dissimilar to the other entities.

Strategies for promoting gender equality in organizations

Succession planning is a big buzz word in promotion management yet without being aware of, and having an intentional methodology to deal with, these conspicuous biases that are below the surface, the best succession planning in the world will fail to promote equitably. In other words, yes it's important to have a deliberate plan for identifying skill gaps (a 360-degree assessment for example) and doubling down on knowledge we see required in staff we lead but, to promote equitably, we need to neutralize as much bias as we can.

A couple of the biases that are going to throw us off every time if we don't deal with them from the start are the *association* bias and one, a recent Mentor Walk mentee experienced blatantly, called *potential versus performance* bias. This is the bias where men are assessed based on their potential and women on their accomplishments. It encapsulates the tendency to evaluate men on the promise of what they might achieve in the future, while women are judged strictly on what they've already accomplished. This might in turn explain why we're gun-shy in promoting women and often feel more comfortable giving responsibility to men (particularly in areas with operational accountabilities). This potential versus performance bias can significantly impact hiring, promotions, and other professional opportunities, leading to disparity in how men and women are perceived and rewarded in various fields.

Like with other biases, the best way to deal with this is to become aware of it, seek out diverse teams to assess candidates for promotion, and intentionally assess the potential AND the accomplishments of the candidates separately and, to the best of your ability, quantifiably (with the caveat to be aware of any intrinsic biases in that quantification).

We need to look beyond what we're used to and challenge our thinking as to why certain things are. Nurture and bring diverse teams together to broaden our perspective about the circumstances and foremost treat the diversity elements (whether it is a male nurse in a sea of female nurses or the one person on an executive board) like diamonds—rare, precious, and sometimes challenging to handle. Ah, the places we'll go if we do.

Chapter summary

Challenging our thinking about our societal norms is key to breaking free of assumptions and supporting each other through adaptive techniques to enable everyone to reach their full potential. By understanding and addressing the specific factors within these societal norms, we can create more inclusive and equitable systems (such as in the example of transport) that cater to the needs of all genders.

Inclusive environments—the right tools

1. **Challenging assumptions**: Initial assumptions about gender-specific traits and roles, such as leadership in crisis situations, may be inaccurate. Research suggests women can be equally effective or even better leaders in crises.

2. **Design for inclusivity**: Environments and tools often favor male physical characteristics and needs. Adapting these for women can lead to better integration and comfort, as illustrated by examples like tailored PPE and ergonomic tools.

3. **Personal story of adaptation**: Real-life experiences highlight the importance of designing tools and equipment that consider women's needs, enabling them to perform tasks effectively and safely.

4. **Human factors in design**: Inclusive design should cater to diverse needs, enabling everyone to pur-

sue any passion or career without unnecessary barriers.

Training on inclusion and diversity

1. **Inclusion as a foundation**: Prioritizing inclusion creates an environment where diversity can thrive. Without inclusion, efforts to hire diverse candidates may fail due to retention issues.

2. **Affinity bias awareness**: Exercises like the Circle of Trust help individuals recognize their biases and encourage them to seek diverse perspectives.

3. **Effective training strategies**:

    - **Interactive formats**: Active participation in workshops and role-playing is more effective than passive learning.

    - **Customized content**: Tailoring training to specific organizational contexts enhances its impact.

    - **Continuous efforts**: Ongoing education and integration into daily practices are essential.

    - **Leadership support**: Both top-down and bottom-up approaches are crucial.

    - **Addressing implicit bias**: Recognizing and mitigating unconscious biases is key.

    - **Measurement and accountability**: Tracking progress and holding individuals accountable ensures effectiveness.

Bias in the workplace

1. **Recognizing bias**: Bias, both conscious and unconscious, can influence decisions and workplace dynamics. Awareness and deliberate actions are required to counteract it.

2. **Practical examples**: Real-life stories (such as hiring practices in STEM fields) illustrate the impact of bias and the need for fair consideration of all candidates.

3. **Neutralizing bias**: Strategies to address bias include:

    o **Groupthink mitigation**: Encouraging diverse viewpoints and using facilitators in discussions.

    o **Fair judgment**: Leaders should withhold judgment until all facts and viewpoints have been considered.

    o **Diverse candidate pools**: Ensuring a mix of candidates without any fundamentally dissimilar entities.

Strategies for promoting gender equality

1. **Succession planning**: Effective promotion management must be deliberate and unbiased, addressing conspicuous biases.

2. **Potential versus performance bias**: Men are often judged on potential, while women on past performance. Awareness and structured assessments can help mitigate this bias.

3. **Diverse assessment teams**: Involving diverse teams in evaluations helps reduce bias and ensure fair consideration.

Conclusion

The key to fostering inclusive and diverse environments lies in challenging assumptions, designing for inclusivity, prioritizing inclusion, and addressing bias through awareness and structured strategies. By treating diversity elements as rare and valuable, organizations can unlock the full potential of their teams, leading to greater innovation, performance, and overall success.

Chapter 5

Balancing Act: Work, Family, and Gender Expectations. It's a societal project for men and women.

There is no such thing as work-life balance- it is all life. The balance has to be within you.

Sadhguru[61]

As a society, we tacitly accept the underutilization, the undervaluation, and the shattering of so many dreams of our young bright minds, and in doing so we leave billions of gross domestic product (GDP) on the table.

It might be revealing for stay-at-home parents to explore, and deeply and candidly consider, the following questions:

- If you had (or currently would have) access to a children development center that would support your child (children), would have the most ad-

vanced brain development tools and methods, offer a warm and healthy lunch designed by a nutritionist, and a speech and language specialist to assure your child's optimal speech development, would you have given up your career and professional passion to stay at home alone with your baby and toddler and figure it all out yourself?
- If you had school transportation for your children that was safe, reliable, and filled with great children their age, driven by a super experienced driver with a tremendous track record and defensive driving training to bring to-and-from school your children, would you have decided to give up your career and professional passion to stay at home to be ready to transport them morning and night?
- If someone told you that statistics show correlation between kids' success in school and life with a stay-at-home parent were at best marginal, and in fact, having dual-career parents might motivate kids to reach their full potential by observing you pursue your own professional aspirations, would you have decided to give up your career to stay at home?[62]
- If your aging parents were being taken care of by trained health and gerontology specialists who were dedicated to helping every day in their own home or in a center. Further that your parents were surrounded with other people their age to socialize, continue to grow, and have fun, would

you have chosen to stay home to take care of them?
- If you were recognized for your contributions and compensated fairly for your work, would you have decided to give up your career and professional passion to stay at home?
- If you knew in a few years you would decide with your partner to give up your career and professional passion to stay at home, would you have invested $80K+ in securing an education and spent multiple years of your life studying?

These questions are difficult and hard to stomach. As a society we've failed all those who'd say "no" to such questions. By not providing true and quality alternatives to our families, we give up on so much potential. This is where we need to rise and solve this challenge better. Until we do so, couples will make suboptimal choices. Not because deep down they want to, but because they believe they have no choice in how to assure the success of their loved ones.

One thing that prompted me to start writing this book was an encounter with an ex-coworker who asked me out for coffee because she needed advice. The first ten or fifteen minutes were simply socializing. We hadn't seen each other in more than a year but gradually she started opening up to me. She shared that while she was very satisfied with her career progress, with a full-time working partner, a child with learning challenges, she wasn't sure the mandate to return to the office five days a week from eight to five was something she was up to. We started to dissect her discomfort. What were the issues? Why were they issues? How could we find innovative solutions to solve them?

My heart went: she is super qualified, super smart, and achieved directorship levels in non-traditional fields. I even knew people in her ecosystem who had reported that she was killing it! How could I help her get unstuck? I was all in design-thinking with her how to break through the barrier(s) to her continuing on her path.

One by one, we dissected:

a) Was she effectively delegating at work?

I shared the three questions I used systematically:

1. Does this task have to be done? If not, then drop it.

    If yes, then

2. Does this task have to be done by me? If not, then delegate it.

    If yes, then

3. Does this task have to be done now? If not, then schedule it.

    If yes, do it now.

We kept on dissecting:

b)   Was she effectively juggling the family world side-by-side with her life partner?

After doubling down on how amazing she was doing, how necessary it was for her to consider how much of an impact she had at work by doing what she was doing, it turned out it was in her personal life where I suggested changes. I invited her to consider tweaks in the way she organized her family commitments. She said she loved dropping her kids off in the morning, but with the imposition of a more rigid back-to-the-office at 100%, it was more difficult. As her child was experiencing learning challenges, she also said they had hired extra help but the specialist's office was far and getting this support meant either her spouse or she had to drive twice a week for a total of nearly three hours. The suggested paradigm shift was as follows, and almost verbatim what I had to do myself a few years prior:

Replace quality time in kind

If you love dropping your kids off but it's no longer possible, ask yourself *What else could I commit to doing with the person (or people) I love just as much?* A weekend Sunday family cook night? A walk after dinner every day of the week? The Saturday family crossword puzzle? Whatever it is that you love. My son and I have this thing that just emerged naturally when I had to drive him to his bass lessons. The road was mainly a highway; not a stop and go type of route. We shared music we loved, new, old, discoveries. Occasionally, I made a detour on the way home, "forgetting" to take the right exit on the highway. He'd look at me with a complicit smile and we both knew we loved this time together. We no longer live in that city and no longer have that drive to make, but we still have the bonding time which I cherish so much. The beauty about our thing is that it's forever new—there's always new music coming out and old music to discover.

Find the help YOU need

There are very many different levels of help. You can send your kids to a school and pay an exorbitant amount for extra support on all fronts and have to drive your kids to it. Or you can pay a little more and send your kids to a school that gives them the help they need. After we returned from Asia, my work was in North America and my spouse was working on a rotation to Dubai for three weeks and three weeks at home. I was juggling the role of being a senior vice president during the day and caring for our children on my own in the evening during the three-week periods my spouse was away. Our kids were both under ten and required a drive in the morning and a pickup at night. This is when we hit the bullseye on the dartboard of chaos.

I'd gone to play squash with my best friend and torn a ligament in my knee. We lived in a three-story house and walking up and down the stairs was something I did every morning trying to get the kids ready for school. I was on my own that week as my spouse had flown off the weekend before. I had to assess and become very vulnerable by asking a girlfriend to move in with me and take care of me and the two kids for the foreseeable future. This was exactly THE help I needed.

Then I received a call at the end of that week informing me my younger brother had passed and suddenly, the ACL injury seemed trivial, and I needed more than just logistical support—I also needed emotional support. This is what I got from the friend who was right there living with us. I'm forever grateful for that period, and I have "gratti-tears" in my eyes thinking about it.

When you find THE help you need; you know it. When you get, or hire help, but you still feel the load (like the example of the extra school support that requires driving three hours a week when you both work full time), then that's not THE help for YOU. Keep looking, become vulnerable, find others who might have similar needs and adopt their solution. Sometimes you'll have to pay more, but it will be small compared to the income you'll make being successful in your career. And the bonus is that you won't have sacrificed anything!

Making it possible for parents to not miss a beat in their career is a societal project and one that we have not finished exploring, particularly for two full-time working spouses. Anecdotes such as the one depicted in the passage from Julie Garland-McLellan, CEO of Director's Dilemma, demonstrate our support systems haven't yet adapted to dual-career parents:

Many childcare providers are focused on the child rather than the mother's career... when I arrived in Sydney as CEO of a multinational energy company's Australian subsidiary, I could get care for a couple of hours one day and three hours another 'until my child was comfortable' and then they would 'see if they could offer more'. Not really appropriate when you work long full days and if I hadn't been able to afford a patchwork of home care (heavily reliant on my husband not being employed) rather than a childcare facility I would not have been able to do my job.[63]

These inadequate societal support services have a direct impact on parents' choice and more often than we would like, an insidious and disproportionate bearing on women:

The price of success for women at work can be high: the average female manager is less likely to be married and more likely to be childless than her male counterpart; half of all women managers are childless, and they are twice as likely to have been divorced or separated as their male colleagues. The majority of male managers' wives were there to be supportive, whilst the majority of female managers were in a dual earner relationship if they were in one at all. The costs of women's caring role in trying to reconcile career and home is well documented. In the light of these experiences, it is no surprise that younger women are emulating the distant role models of successful female managers and are being much more circumspect about when and whether to have children.[64]

The importance of finding THE right help

There are so many women with professional careers who decide to stay home with their kids. For a variety of reasons, it seems to be one area that's not politically correct to challenge these days. It is an intertwined and existential question and is loaded with "guilt-if-you-do, guilt-if-you-don't."

My hope is that as a society we find ways to support every single woman and man in their pursuit and make it the obvious choice for them all to continue to contribute to the prosperity of our society, our world, to knock it out of the park, and to reach their absolute potential. This path, where we completely and unconditionally give the tools, options, and encouragement needed to make it a no-brainer for everyone to pursue their passion and career aspiration, will yield reaching heights we haven't seen yet in our lifetime. It will inevitably reduce:

- depression (because we feel underutilized with limited mental challenges, and with limited recognition for what we do)
- addiction (the go-to self-medication for deep-seated unhappiness that can't be resolved because we don't have the means, the opportunity to shine, the feeling of worthiness that everyone deserves)
- divorce (because couples will be able to both feel fulfilled with their pursuits and supported by the society, their family, their partner in their pursuits)
- families falling apart (because the more satisfied you are with yourself, the more open you'll be to supporting others)
- feelings of not belonging (because you'll need a village to succeed in your pursuits and the only way to get there is to accept the vulnerability of speaking up when you need help. You'll find that if supporting each other becomes the norm, you'll lean in too!)

There are many physical and circumstantial factors affecting the decision of a couple to have one of the partners stay home with the kids. These factors can be broadly categorized into economic, personal, social, and logistical considerations:

Economic factors

- **Income disparity**: If one spouse earns significantly more than the other, it often makes financial sense for the lower-earning spouse to stay home. The gut feeling that the lower-income parent should stay home to assure the success of the family (by doing laundry, picking up the kids from school, preparing hot meals, going to appointments, attending teachers-parents' interviews, doing homework) is often in actuality the sabotage of a sparked and quality relationship. The destruction of someone's mental growth and pursuits, leading to sadness and perhaps depression in later years. The dissonant impact on our children who see everything and might conclude it's OK not to challenge ourselves to help the productive aspects of our society to the maximum of our potential! It's also giving up on our self-esteem and a lifetime of pondering what could have been if I'd continued to pursue my passion. Staying at home is a short-term compromise, and perhaps a short-term financial advantage depending on your salary and environment and affordability of help. For the long-term, it has the real potential of being an emotional and financial loss.

- **Childcare costs**: The high cost of childcare can make it economically advantageous for one parent to stay home, especially if the cost of childcare would consume a large portion of their salary. This is where we need to help as a society. I was six months pregnant with my first one when I was laughed at by the day care attendant pointing out to me that I was late-to-the-game trying to find a day care for a service I needed six months down the road. That is way more angst than needed—where there's a will there is a way. For everyone's sake, we must find a solution to the societal conundrum of how we provide everyone (including low-income families) the support they need to pursue their careers.

Personal factors

- **Parental preference**: A personal desire to be involved in child-rearing is a significant factor. Some parents prioritize being present during their children's early years.

- **Job satisfaction**: If one spouse has lower job satisfaction, they might be more willing to stay home.

- **Career flexibility**: Careers that allow for part-time work or flexible hours can influence the decision. A less flexible career might push one spouse to stay home.

Social factors

- **Cultural norms and values**: Societal and cultural expectations can play a significant role. In some cultures, there's a stronger emphasis on one parent (often the mother) staying home with children.

- **Support systems**: Availability of support from extended family and community can affect the decision. Families with strong support systems might feel more comfortable having both parents' work.

- **Peer influence**: Couples might be influenced by their friends' and relatives' decisions and experiences regarding stay-at-home parenting.

Logistical factors

- **Work commute and hours**: Long work hours and commutes can make balancing a career and parenting difficult, tipping the decision towards one parent staying home.

- **Number and age of children**: Families with multiple young children may find it more practical for one parent to stay home.

- **Health considerations**: Health issues of either the parent or the child can necessitate a stay-at-home parent.

Additional considerations

- **Future career prospects**: The potential long-term career impact for the stay-at-home parent is often considered. Taking a break can affect future job opportunities and career progression.

- **Retirement and benefits**: Couples often weigh the impact of one spouse not working on retirement savings and benefits such as health insurance.

The decision for one spouse to stay at home with the kids rather than returning to a career is multi-faceted, involving a complex interplay of economic, personal, social, and logistical factors. Each family's situation is unique, and what works for one may not be suitable for another. Equality partnership, when both income earning duties and home duties are shared, leads to happier relationships according to research.[65] As Sheryl Sandberg says in her book *Lean-In*, "When women work outside the home and share breadwinning duties, couples are more likely to stay together. In fact, the risk of divorce reduces by about half when a wife earns at least half of the income, and a husband does half the housework."[66] Furthermore, "children who were cared for exclusively by their mothers did not develop differently than those who were also cared for by others."[67] The research Sandberg revealed to us more than ten years ago also identified no gap in cognitive skills, language competence, social competence, ability to build and maintain relationships, or in the quality of the mother-child bond. The quality of the parents' relationship seems to have multiple folds more of a positive effect than childcare experiences.[68] This is a compelling incentive for us to focus on nurturing our attraction and enthusiasm for our life together as we go through the parenting years with our life partner.

Highlighted in this research is the fact the quality of the childcare mattered, hence our need to focus on

THE support we need as parents. Our societal fabric should be augmented to the point where all parents trust and know their kids are given all the help they need to thrive, grow, and develop to reach their full potential! Until we can be rest assured the child needs are met, the psychological burden of feeling you've done a subpar job as a parent will be with us while that should NOT be the case.

Until recently, I held quite a bit of angst about the fact that my daughter was behind in reading and writing for her grade. Because we have international careers, we'd moved the kids many times in their early years. After my second parental leave, when my daughter was ten months old, we moved to Indonesia for four years. I was working long hours, and we'd hired staff for help. We also speak two languages as a couple: I speak French with the kids while my spouse speaks English. Things get complicated when you move to a country where neither of these languages are broadly spoken.

My daughter's formative years were spent exposed to Bahasa Indonesia for about ten hours a day during business days, with about twenty hours hearing English from conversations between my spouse and I and my spouse speaking with her, and maybe five to ten hours of one-on-one French with me. Fast forward to Grade 4 and she was behind in French and English reading and writing.

In our last move, I literally started crying when the admission person, at the school we were hoping to get in, had an introductory meeting with us. The very nice admission person, after giving my daughter and I a tour of the school, explained to me, "Don't worry, we've got this." They went on to describe: "Our students, while they come to us with challenges, if we support them early enough (and they assured me Grade 5 was early enough), the students at the school graduate Grade 12 at the same rate as all the others in the country."

In my heart I knew this was THE help we needed, and I literally had to have the tissue box passed to me. I deeply hoped we'd be accepted to start in September. We ultimately did get accepted, and we were (and still are) beyond grateful for the highly qualified and supporting staff.

Until recently, I thought it was a luxury for couples to decide to have a parent at home raising the kids (most of my peers were in that situation, especially as I climbed up to more senior ranks). I also believed the odds of success of kids with one parent looking after them with focus would be way better. I was surprised to discover that it doesn't make any difference statistically. In fact, boys and girls with mom working seem to be more inspired to be considered for sharing the workload at home and inspired to consider advanced careers. Sheryl Sandberg highlighted this study which helped me greatly come to terms with our choice to be a dual-career couple; I'm infinitely grateful to Ms. Sandberg for picking up her pen to inform us all.[69] I'm a career-loving parent and hope more will consider doing the same.

Finally, I always reflected on the fact that my mom had, for the lion's share of my growing up, a full-time job and business responsibilities, and many nannies took good care of us when we were young. I've lost touch with almost all the nannies, but the love and attachment I have for my mom and her presence in my life as a strong advocate, supporter, and advisor has never been affected by her choice. We're very close, and I trust and deep down know that even if I have a high-intensity career and pursuits to better our world, my children will feel connected to me always just the same.

Chapter summary

This chapter delves into the complex interplay between work, family responsibilities, and gender expectations, emphasizing this balancing act is a societal issue affecting both men and women. Here are the key takeaways:
- **Societal cost of underutilization**: The chapter begins by highlighting the societal acceptance of underutilizing and undervaluing talented individuals, which leads to significant economic losses. The potential of young, bright minds is often wasted, leaving billions in GDP untapped.

- **Challenging traditional roles**: It questions traditional gender roles and the expectation for one parent, typically the mother, to stay home. Through a series of introspective questions, it challenges readers to reconsider if they would choose to stay home if high-quality childcare and eldercare options were available.
- **Decision factors for stay-at-home parents**: Several factors influencing the decision for one parent to stay home are discussed, including access to quality childcare, reliable transportation for children, eldercare support, and recognition and fair compensation in the workplace.
- **Personal anecdotes and solutions**: I share a personal story of helping a former colleague navigate her discomfort with returning to a rigid work schedule post-pandemic. We dissect her issues and explore practical solutions, such as effective delegation, reorganizing family commitments, and finding alternative quality time with children.
- **Importance of THE right help**: Emphasizes finding the right kind of help, whether it's childcare, eldercare, or logistical support, to enable parents to continue their professional pursuits without feeling overwhelmed. The story of my own experience with balancing a demanding career and family life underscores this point.
- **Societal support systems**: The chapter advocates for societal changes to provide better support sys-

tems for working parents. Examples include accessible, high-quality childcare and flexible work arrangements, which can alleviate the pressure on parents and allow them to pursue their careers without compromising their family's well-being.
- **Impact on children's development**: Research is presented showing that children of working parents don't fare worse than those with stay-at-home parents. In fact, the quality of the parent-child relationship and the support system in place play a more crucial role in a child's development.
- **Economic and personal benefits of dual-career families**: Dual-career families often experience lower divorce rates and higher relationship satisfaction. Children in these families may also benefit from seeing both parents engaged in fulfilling careers.
- **Encouragement for career-loving parents**: The chapter encourages parents to embrace their professional passions and assures them that, with the right support, it's possible to have a successful career and a fulfilling family life. It challenges societal norms that guilt parents, particularly mothers, for pursuing careers.
- **Future prospects and cultural shift**: Advocates for a cultural shift towards supporting all parents in their professional and personal aspirations, ultimately leading to a more prosperous and balanced society.

In conclusion, the chapter calls for a societal re-evaluation of how we support families, urging for better infrastructure and cultural acceptance to enable both men and women to pursue their careers without sacrificing their family life. The goal is to reach a point where the decision to stay home or work is based on genuine choice rather than necessity.

Chapter 6

Effective Communication Across Diversity Lines

Just because you carry it well, [it] doesn't mean it isn't heavy.

Inspiration board at HotYoga17[70]

As the two of us were driving back from the mountains one weekend, I asked my spouse what he appreciated about the quality of our communication. As life partners, one of the things we navigate is stark differences in culture. While we're from the same country, we grew up speaking a different language, were exposed to different kids' shows and music (when we met, I knew only 10% of his music downloads and he knew even less of mine), have unquestionably opposed senses of humor, and on and on. We do share, however, the same undergrad studies; both of us were provincially ranked at squash (which is how we met) and at the root of it all our top two values: health and growth.

My father-in-law, who is astute and has a great sense of observation, always says to us that he's rarely seen a couple sorting things out together the way we do; he says we have an efficient approach to resolving standstills. He's seen us negotiate many life decisions over the years: where to live in a different country, where to send our kids to school, and how we were intentional about our time allocation as a family to ensure everyone's social and development needs were met.

Prior to meeting my spouse, I tended to be subpar at sharing how I felt in my personal life. This turned around when I met Colin. He brought our communication together to a whole new level. At one point he asked me a personal question and my answer was, "I haven't even asked myself that question yet!". To this day we laugh at this early period where I was less than adequate at personal sharing. I had to take baby steps, but they came with a desire and intention to get better. Specifically, I didn't want to repeat the experience of my first marriage, which ended in divorce. My ex-spouse was taken by surprise the day I left because I hadn't kept the "lens" clean. I had bottled up frustrations I hadn't shared, perhaps because I'd clumsily tried to share my dissatisfaction in our relationship and had been ignored or met with resistance. In a nutshell, I'd given up.

My analogy for my mental model when it comes to getting better at communicating is about the concept of a *lens*. The lens is clean when you meet each other (unless the relationship is already tainted by a bad reputation), and it must be intentional to keep it clean. Think about how clean the lens is when you're floating on cloud nine in love, and you see everything about your partner through rose-tinted glasses. It's not because the person you're with is a god or goddess; it's because your lens is clear of all the little things that might bother you. Over the years, if you don't cultivate authentic and difficult conversations in a positive way, the lens will get foggy and soiled. If, on the other hand, you work together to ensure the lens stays clean, you'll most likely see your relationship evolve positively and even blossom—blossom because you appreciate both the desire of your partner to grow and your own growth.

To keep the lens clean, you need to be authentic with each other. If you feel something, share it—good or bad. If it's good, double down on the sharing and explain why. If it's bad, double down on a considerate, tender, and light delivery. In my operational lingo, whenever we did safety walks, the motto was "If you see it, you own it." That means if we saw something unsafe or hazardous (in this case "unsafe" for the relationship), we had to either fix it right away, delegate someone else to fix it right away, or enter the observation in a database for awareness and for a plan to be established to fix it. In the same vein with communication across diverse lines, if you disagree with something or you dislike it, you're accountable for finding a way to fix it, whether it requires a swift and easy nudge, a long conversation over dinner, or a six-month plan assisted by a therapist.

Context 1: Across diversity lines at work

Communication is a very human and fundamental need. Communication across diversity lines requires extra attention and patience before you can become comfortable with it. It's common to find it easier to communicate with your own types (think about boys' or girls' nights out). There's a lot of social conditioning that comes with this construct and gender-discriminating circles or associations. Indirectly, based on my observations, it often results in the minority feeling (or literally being) left out. When there's an effort made to muster the discomfort that might come from inviting a minority to join in, it often results in tremendous gratitude and benefits all. In particular, it allows for more appreciation and the organic creation of allyships.

To positively transform our workplaces, we need to start by being intentional and welcoming the possible discomfort that comes from communicating across the diversity lines. Diversity might come with challenges, but in the long run it pays off. We need to be lenient, patient, and—most importantly—listen deeply to the people around us. Putting people together to solve problems collaboratively, and favoring human interaction over written communication whenever possible, can help to remove some of the inhibitors to quality communication.

CONCLUSION 1: Build bridges and embrace the discomfort to benefit from diversity in the long run.

Context 2: Find allies in your peer group

Another attribute to quality communication is to observe in your environment who you trust. The best person might not be the person you think of first. On multiple occasions, as I was the minority at the table (often one woman in ten or twelve people), I engaged allies to help me navigate the challenges that might come ahead. I was often proactive about this, particularly in multi-engagement settings such as weekly leadership meetings, quarterly negotiation meetings, partners meetings, long-term clients' meetings. I would make a point of having an offline conversation with one ally who might have shown skills in bringing people together and were emotionally astute and aware at the table. I would ask them directly, if they would be so kind as to be on the lookout for dynamics that might be sub-optimal in my communication style, interventions from my end that were not received well, or comments that might have fallen flat for the audience/team. I would openly and with humility share that I was a minority at the table, and it would greatly help me navigate if they would graciously accept to make me aware of these communication mishaps so I could improve over time. If appropriate, I would also ask them to take aside co-workers who were struggling with me due to their unconscious biases dealing with a woman.

Someone else at the table having your back is tremendously helpful and is something we need to actively seek; in some ways even more so than traditional mentors because your mentors will rarely see you in action while your co-workers will all the time. They can often naturally intervene early before communication problems become real issues. Often, by showing that vulnerability to one person, I would gain tremendous allies: allies I could go to even after we stopped being at the same table. I recommend finding allies in your peer group, rather than a boss or a report, especially at the senior level. A funny anecdote is the day I went to my boss to tell him I was overloaded. To my surprise, in lieu of helping me figure things out, he sternly clarified that I was a senior leader and had to figure out how I could do the load. I was accountable for finding THE help I needed. He was not kidding and was not going to solve my problem for me. I felt that day, I had graduated to the big people league, i.e., I had become a fully fledged predominant creator of my "work" life. My lesson then was to help my boss out rather than adding to their load—the more senior you are, the more viable this is. Err on the safe side and think, *how can I find allies in my peers and how can I help my boss succeed?*

CONCLUSION 2: Find communication allies, and as you climb the corporate ladder, focus on enabling your boss to succeed.

Context 3: Understand your audience well and align on principles

This might seem like a Communication 101 lesson, but it's one that requires a lot of practice. You'll find yourself in environments where you're the minority, in which case it's imperative that you seek to understand your audience, even do pre-engagement research to ensure you don't make an unnecessary faux pas. The same goes for a group wanting to succeed in making a person who might be different from the majority fit in and feel included.

One technique I love to use to seek to understand the thinking of the audience (whether in personal or professional life) is the concept of *alignment on key principles*. Explore the points and objectives you have in common and try to articulate these principles in words or even better in writing. For example, my spouse and I have in common the values of health and growth. Between us, these are treated as *principles,* because when either of us plans something related to these two aligned values, the support and understanding we mutually feel and the encouragement we give each other in these two areas really helps converge quickly on priorities.

A business example was when I worked in Asia and was the chair of a main conglomerate of shippers. The legal agreements we had between us had been a source of confusion, even discord, for years. As a group of shippers, we managed to get out of the impasse by aligning on a dozen principles which were put in writing. We ultimately created a standard operating procedure, to supplement the operating agreement in effect, which lifted the deadlock. These long negotiations across diversity lines resolved the problem sustainably, as all of us understood better where the other parties at the table were coming from.

CONCLUSION 3: Seek to understand and align on key principles between parties.

Chapter summary

In "Just Because You Carry It Well, Doesn't Mean It Isn't Heavy," we delve into the nuanced world of communication across diverse lines, encompassing not only gender but also cultural, linguistic, and personal differences. This chapter unveils the complexities and rewards of bridging these gaps through intentional, authentic, and strategic communication.

A personal journey of cultural differences

I invite you into an intimate narrative describing how

I was driving back from a serene mountain trip, pondering the essence of quality communication with my spouse. Despite sharing a nationality, our upbringings in different cultural and linguistic environments shaped our distinct perspectives. This section highlights the importance of shared values—in this case, health and growth—in navigating and appreciating these differences. My journey from subpar personal sharing to a deeper, more effective communication style underlines the transformative power of intentional efforts and vulnerability.

Clean lens metaphor

A compelling metaphor used throughout the chapter is the "clean lens." When relationships begin, our lens is clear, and we see the best in our partners. However, over time, without authentic and often challenging conversation, this lens can become clouded. Keeping the lens clean involves honest communication—expressing both good and bad feelings with care and tenderness. Acknowledging and addressing issues immediately, akin to a safety walk's proactive approach, is crucial in maintaining clear, healthy communication lines.

Contextual insights on communication

1. **Diversity in the workplace:** I stress the need for intentionality and patience in communication across diverse lines at work. Embracing the discomfort of these interactions ultimately leads to a

richer, more collaborative environment. Encouraging human interaction over written communication can break down barriers and foster inclusivity.

2. **Finding allies:** Building a network of allies within your peer group, especially in senior positions, is pivotal. My own experience of seeking support from colleagues rather than superiors highlights the value of peer relationships. This approach helps us to navigate challenges and fosters a supportive and inclusive work environment.

3. **Understanding your audience:** Aligning on key principles with your audience is essential. Whether in personal or professional settings, understanding and articulating shared values and objectives can prevent misunderstanding and build stronger connections. I provide examples from both my personal and professional lives, illustrating the effectiveness of this strategy.

Conclusion

"Just because you carry it well, doesn't mean it isn't heavy" imparts a crucial lesson: effective communication across diverse lines requires continuous effort, authenticity, and strategic alignment. By maintaining a clean lens, finding allies, and understanding our audience, we can navigate the complexities of diversity with grace and reap the long-term benefits of enriched, meaningful relationships.

Chapter 7

Thriving Together: Participative Decision-Making

Power is not coercive; it simply directs the flow of energy. Force always moves against something, whereas power doesn't move against anything at all.

David R. Hawkins[71]

How can we eliminate the barriers to participative decision-making in the context of diversity? And further, how can we leverage diversity for better outcomes by providing valued experiences for all? There's a personal story which transformed my career. I was working in Houston as a senior engineer in the head office corporate planning group. I'd been involved with the senior executives of this multibillion-dollar organization over three years. We were allowed in the CEO meetings as resources and would sit behind the decision makers in a "gallery" style. We were the go-to for financial and engineering details associated with the company's plan and forecast. It was a tremendous privilege to be able to see firsthand decision-making in action at the highest level. I was young, enthusiastic, and a quick learner, and I was treated well. Salaries were the best in the industry, and we were attracting people who'd studied at the best schools. I even traveled on the corporate jet with the executive team to visit business units.

I was a bit intimidated when the CFO invited me to join their poker game; not because I didn't know how to play but because I was thinking, *What if I lose and they think I don't belong?* I politely declined. To this day I wish I could tell my younger self, *Be courageous and try it.* Despite my lack of participation in the poker game, I'd built a great reputation as a diligent and strategic contributor to the company's performance and helped with sorting out what portfolio would best meet the corporate objectives and analyzed many what-if scenarios when decisions were too complex to assess without a mathematical model. I was working extra-long hours, even sometimes on my days off, but I was having fun. I was growing, building resilience and skills, and was exposed to a world (decision sciences) which is to this day one of the most exciting explorations of my career. My role at the time had fewer engineering components and much more finance aspects, so although working long hours, I decided to sign up for a graduate certificate in finance and accounting—why not? Attending Rice University was the opportunity of a lifetime.

I had no budget accountabilities back then, as my role served as an interface between the executive team and the business units. To use an offshore analogy, it was the equivalent of being a quick connect and disconnect (QCDC) system on a ship; everything went through us and our team was at the center between strategy and execution, yet we never signed any cheques nor had the authority to commit the company to anything. It was a perfect training ground for any aspiring leader. I'd been promoted to the role because I'd complained about the convolutedness of our planning process.

A few months later my boss had walked into my office saying, "You've been telling me the corporate long range planning process is broken. Go and fix it! There's a perfect job that seems to be made just for you at head office!"

The next thing I knew, I was moving to a different country! More than three years went by, then came time to be repatriated to my home business unit, where I was offered the respectable role of strategic planning manager. I guess most people would have been delighted with the assignment—I wasn't. It wasn't because it wasn't a great role, or because I didn't love strategic planning, but because every single person before me in the role I'd been in for nearly four years had been given significant P&L accountabilities when they came out of it successfully. But I was offered a support role (no operations and no budget).

- I remember embracing the discomfort of having to stand up for myself, took my courage in my hands, and went to my boss with the strategic planning manager job description. My voice was shaking, and I felt as if I might burst into tears when I highlighted the disparity—it was so unfair. I said, "Thank you for offering the area planning managerial position but I need to have a chat."

- He immediately said, "This is a fabulous role where you'll have significant influence."

- "But I'm a mechanical engineer," I responded, "and all the gentlemen before me had sunk their teeth in significant project leadership after their QCDC roles. Could the company reconsider and find me a role with more budgetary accountabilities?"

To my elation the leadership team did, and this reconsideration changed the course of my career! They gave me the biggest program in the business unit with the most capital, and I led one of the largest development teams. This was THE moment when everything changed. I was invited to all the regional leaders' meetings and asked by many junior women for help in their career development. And because I'm a technically inclined leader, I gained the support of the most senior professionals in the business unit. I was leading people who were nearly twenty years my senior. I had a coach and did 360 surveys to help grow my leadership awareness, but what helped the most was that weekly coffee with my still close friends to this day—Fred and John. They gave me the true and authentic account as to what was going on, who needed help with understanding the objectives, and which partnerships we needed to make outside the team. They were two of the most senior people on my team and because I sought their knowledge and expertise, they took me under their wing. What wings they gave me! Two years later we had multiple big wins back-to-back and almost became known as the heavy hitters' team.

After successfully completing this leadership position, spending the biggest piece of the business unit capital over multiple years, and leading a team that really liked me as a leader, I was given increasingly greater responsibility. I was sent on the expat international circuit, and ultimately led a region with a net profit of over $1 billion a year.

You need to learn the ropes and you need to step up and embrace the discomfort of negotiating for accountabilities—especially budgetary accountabilities. When you're in charge of a budget, and have approval authority over it, you don't just influence, you also have a direct impact on the performance of an asset or a team. If you're in a minority situation in your organization, be intentional about seeking roles that have that direct impact on the value rather than an indirect "influence" type of impact. These roles come with complexity, politics, and hoops to jump through, and there's no free lunch. Yet, the long-term reward in your heart, the pride, the difference you make, and the financial windfall for having stepped up and applied your best self is an utterly rewarding feeling. Short-term discomfort is beyond worth it.

What I experienced that day, when I was given my first significant budget, is now coined *participative decision-making* in diversity lingo. The United Nations subsidiary UN Women published an article called "Gender Equality Accelerators" last year.[72] It highlights the ten Gender Equality Accelerators and, among other things, the top one: Women's Equal Participation in Political (and Economic) Decision-Making and Institutions.

The message at the UN Sustainable Development Goals summit in September 2023 was crystal clear: the world is failing to achieve gender equality, making it an increasingly distant goal. The sense of urgency is sharp. The state of gender equality and women's rights needs strategic, coordinated action.

As a response to this challenge, UN Women has worked with key partners to identify the root causes of persisting inequality and the most pressing issues for women and girls. The 10 Gender Equality Accelerators offer essential solutions to overcome existing challenges in achieving women and girls' human rights and sustainability and development goal #5, (SDG 5), pertaining to gender equality.[73]

The power of shared decision-making is essential to successfully leverage diverse perspectives for better outcomes. Implementing effective decision-making processes is about looking at alternatives through various lenses to innovatively reveal real solutions to achieving our common goals and objectives. We need to embrace the discomfort of changing the narrative and provide meaningful training grounds for our professionals, even those who don't look the same or seem different as all their predecessors in a role. And you need to give them the authority and associated accountability that comes from the direct influence of your profit line.

Chapter summary

In this chapter, the focus shifts from the general field of decision sciences to the practical application of participative decision-making within diverse environments. The key takeaway is the significance of eliminating barriers to inclusive decision-making to leverage diverse perspectives for superior outcomes.

Personal journey and career transformation

- **Early career in Houston:** I share a pivotal personal story, detailing my journey as a senior engineer involved in corporate planning at a major organization. Engaging with senior executives and participating in high-level decision-making provided invaluable exposure early in my career.

- **Overcoming intimidation:** Despite initial hesitation, such as declining a poker game with the CFO, I built a solid reputation through hard work and strategic contributions, often working long hours and investing in further education at Rice University.

- **Promotion and new challenges:** Recognized for my critical observations about the company's planning process, I was promoted and relocated, and I thrived in a role that served as a bridge between strategy and execution. This experience highlighted the importance of advocacy and seizing opportunities for growth.

Negotiating for accountability

- **Facing career disparities:** Upon returning to the home business unit, I encountered a potential setback when offered a support role lacking budgetary responsibilities, unlike my predecessors.

- **Advocacy and courage:** Demonstrating courage, I negotiated for a more impactful role, ultimately securing a leadership position with significant budgetary accountability. This decision transformed my career, leading to increased leadership opportunities.

Lessons learned

- **Importance of direct impact roles:** I emphasize that roles with budgetary accountability offer greater influence and direct impact on organizational performance, which is crucial for career advancement, especially for individuals in minority situations.

- **Embracing complexity and discomfort:** Such roles often involve complexity and politics, but the long-term rewards—both personal and professional—are significant.

Participative decision-making and gender equality

- **Participative decision-making:** The concept (in my experience) involves inclusive and shared decision-making processes, crucial for leveraging diverse perspectives.

- **UN women's gender equality accelerators:** Highlighting the urgency of gender equality, this chapter references UN Women's initiatives aimed at overcoming persistent inequalities and promoting women's participation in decision-making.

Conclusion:

- **Power of shared decision-making:** Effective decision-making processes require considering diverse alternatives to achieve common goals. This approach necessitates changing traditional narratives and providing meaningful opportunities for all professionals, including those from diverse backgrounds.

- **Authority and accountability:** For true participative decision-making, professionals must be given the authority and accountability to influence outcomes directly, ensuring that diversity leads to tangible improvements in organizational performance and equality.

Embracing diversity and participative decision-making is not only a matter of fairness but also a strategic advantage that can drive better outcomes and foster a more inclusive workplace.

Chapter 8

Resolving Conflict and Negotiating Empowering Solutions

Act the way you would like to be and pretty soon you'll be the way you act.

Leonard Cohen[74]

In the realm of negotiations, understanding the distinctive traits and strategies employed by men and women can be the key to unlocking successful outcomes. Helping both genders find a winning approach to negotiation AND come with an open-and-aware stance vis-à-vis who is across the table, are stepping stones towards equity. Roger Greenfield, Partner at The GAP Partnership, is one of the best negotiators I've ever encountered. I had the pleasure of working with him during a multi-billion-dollar transaction we successfully negotiated in the Asia-Pacific region. We sporadically stayed connected thereafter, and he graciously agreed to give me an interview. During the conversation, I explored the nuances that differentiate male and female negotiators. Our discussion highlighted critical insights into how gender influences negotiation styles, the role of ego and assertiveness, and the unique strengths women and men bring to the table. Roger and I wanted to explore broad generalizations in the propensities of the genders when it comes to observations, and in some cases, research. While I usually dislike generalizations, they do help explore and test if we have opportunities to adopt approaches that might feel uncomfortable at first but could significantly improve our craft in the long run. It's essential to recognize these are broad tendencies and not absolute rules—individual differences can vary widely. Exploring our propensity when we enter negotiations, what strengths come naturally, and what aspects are causing frustration and unease are all elements to evolve on the path of mastery. While negotiations will never be easy, with practice and trying on-for-size different tactics, you might find yourself navigating them with ease.

Ego and competitive behavior

Through our chat, we explored why we regularly saw men perceive powerful women as threats, which can heighten their competitive behavior.

Greenfield said:

You know there is a piece about ego and the role that your ego plays in a negotiation. From a man's perspective, very often they see a powerful woman or a senior woman as a threat and therefore that sort of spikes or pricks their ego a little bit more. That unfortunately produces more competitive behavior. In my experience, this ego is less evident in women who are more likely to use approaches that will drive stronger collaboration. Collaboration then feeds into exploring and understanding needs better and then driving more creative solutions. As a generalized tendency, the masculine approach tends to be a bit more of a blunt instrument, which is at its extreme: I'm just going to use my power to hammer you into the ground and make you agree with what I want you to agree with. I don't know how much of that is a conscious or even a subconscious thing for men.

In certain instances, there might be an advantage for more aggressive, power-based negotiation tactics. In contrast, other instances might benefit from influences fostering collaboration and understanding, leading to more creative and mutually beneficial solutions. You must assess and strategize on the approach that has the potential to land the best negotiated outcomes. Through tailored preparation and coaching, men and women can grow new, more sophisticated skills and keep unfavorable tendencies in check—and this is true for both genders.

Collaboration and creativity

I shared my experience, noting that I approach negotiations with a *seek to understand and help others to do the same* mindset. This often results in less conflict and more successful outcomes. Greenfield concurred, emphasizing that women excel in driving collaboration, which is essential for exploring and understanding needs better and generating innovative solutions. I also shared my shadow side, which is a need for transparent negotiations where hidden agendas are kept to a minimum. Sometimes I feel unsettled, not knowing how to behave, in more confrontational negotiations. Being aware of these limitations is important when it comes to being prepared. Knowing that propensity going in, I focus on objectivity, breathing, and equanimity. I capitalize on framing my ask and listening deeply to evolve a creative solution that helps build as many bridges as possible between parties. Negotiations can become emotional and knowing the mindset that will neutralize the fear or vulnerability, is important when it comes to being prepared.

We then explored how in the creativity department, male negotiators may be more likely to think outside the box, propose unconventional or bold solutions. This could be attributed to a willingness to take risks or to challenge existing norms. When in a minority situation however, I observe this trait is often difficult to daringly exhibit, as you might be perceived as challenging the status-quo. Digging in for a tactful and considerate delivery is, in many cases, a catalyst to enabling breakthrough moments.

All in all, we concluded the best negotiators were the ones able to collaborate to reveal the collective knowledge to ultimately yield creative solutions.

Assertiveness and negotiation outcomes

Assertiveness emerged as a pivotal trait in negotiations. Greenfield observed that men are typically more assertive, a factor that contributes to their higher likelihood of anchoring negotiations in their favor and pushing their agendas more forcefully. Women tend to be less assertive, which can affect their negotiation outcomes. Greenfield suggested that enhancing assertiveness in women could improve their negotiation effectiveness. I noted there might be an inherent reason for observing a tendency in women to be less assertive. In fact, in my experience unless I used specific softening words in tough negotiations, assertiveness would backfire whereas things might get more confrontational than I would have liked. In turn, it brought the interaction in a direction I felt less at ease in.

Confidence and counterproposals

Greenfield emphasized the importance of confidence for women in negotiations. He advised that women should feel empowered to counter-propose rather than accepting initial offers. This assertiveness in offering alternatives can lead to better negotiation outcomes. He also highlighted the significance of exploring options and building trust, which are areas where women typically excel. I observed that it was much easier to counter-propose, in the construct of a business negotiation, rather than when I negotiated for myself. Intuitively, it is much easier to separate yourself from the problem when it's not personal. After investigating this paradox, which is expressed by the adage: "One must be a shoemaker to have poorly fitting shoes", I concluded the solution lies in augmented framing[75].

1. Preparation and planning: Analyze past negotiation outcomes and industry benchmarks to quantify the value of your counterproposal and anticipate potential objections.

2. Clarification and justification: Use specific metrics and data points to articulate a counterproposal. This helps to corroborate how it meets or exceeds key performance indicators relevant to the negotiation.

3. Bargaining and problem solving: Don't hesitate to pull out an excel sheet and play out the what-if scenarios. Applying quantitative modeling to evaluate the potential impact of various solutions, using probabilities to predict outcomes and guide the negotiation towards the most beneficial result. It can also provide extra insight to smoothly arrive at a balanced position.

4. Closure and implementation: This is the place where many counterproposals fall short, particularly in non-business circumstances. Document agreed terms thoroughly and involve legal councils even if, in the moment, it seems like an overkill. Include relevant figures and milestones to ensure clear accountability and measurable progress during implementation.

Emotional intelligence

The conversation also touched on the role of emotional intelligence in negotiations. Greenfield noted that cultivating a grasp of emotional influencing, can be a powerful tool. The good news is that there seems to be no significant difference between the genders on their total score measuring emotional intelligence, but the genders did tend to differ in emotional self-awareness, interpersonal relationships, and empathy with women scoring higher than men[76]. By leveraging their understanding of emotions, women and men can enhance their ability to influence and negotiate effectively. Emotional intelligence, or sometimes also called EQ or emotional quotient, is a superpower and perhaps one of the most difficult to develop as it's arduous to measure its progress. In other words, it's the sum of a lot of abstract constructs such as social skills, social awareness, self-regulation, and self awareness[77]. Observing who on your team has it naturally, ensuring they're in the most crucial conversations, and most importantly taking cues from these individuals, might be the best way to bridge EQ gaps.

Practical advice for women negotiators

Towards the end of our discussion, I asked Greenfield for specific advice for women entering negotiations. His key recommendations were:

- **Have the confidence to counter-propose:** Women shouldn't accept the first offer but instead feel confident to present counterproposals.

- **Use collaborative techniques:** Women should capitalize on their strength in collaboration, exploring creative solutions, and building trust with other party.

- **Be lenient with yourself:** Above all, women should continue to strive for improvement in their negotiation skills yet they should also consider that unconscious biases are still lying below the surface of what we understand today. Studies are constantly coming out revealing systematic inequities needing to be neutralized.

Our conversation shed light on the distinctive strengths and challenges faced by men and women in negotiations. By understanding these dynamics, negotiators can adopt strategies. Specifically, they can harness the collaborative and empathetic approaches often seen in women (while also finding ways to enhance the assertiveness and confidence often seen in men) to drive better negotiation outcomes for all. This advice is useful, and every attempt to integrate it in an approach will yield improvement.

A recent study reveals "Now, Women Do Ask: A call to Update Beliefs about the Gender Pay Gap."[78] In their article, based on a sample of 3,374 business administration students and alumni, the authors highlight that women have taken the push to negotiate in stride to the point they might have changed the statistics. This is particularly true around pay negotiation, where 54% of women indicated they negotiated while only 44% of men did the same. Despite women negotiating more than their male counterparts, the researchers found that women were still paid significantly less than men. "Therefore, the pay gap in this population disfavoring women cannot logically be due to women not asking," the researchers conclude.[79] Instead of asserting women *do not ask* we needed to replace the assertion with women are *punished for asking*. However, it's important to do both—encourage everyone to negotiate adopting strategies that have high probability to be successful for them AND, as a society, continue to seek to understand and reveal biases and barriers attributable to gender or through being part of another minority so they can be neutralized and removed. Women and minority individuals are doing their part to progress on the path of equity. They will continue to try as hard as they can but let's be sure we don't expect those experiencing discrimination to bear the weight of resolving issues and bridging all the gaps on their shoulders.

Gender propensity and opportunities

Many opportunities exist in a course of significant multi-party negotiations to strategically place the members of the negotiation team in counterparty engagements. Understanding the various negotiation traits found in the gender archetypes doesn't mean that individuals aren't capable of building skills that might not be their natural tendencies. With proper mindset preparation, qualitative and quantitative positioning, and proper alliances, your head negotiator (whether a man or woman) will have the significant elements to succeed.

When I arrived in Indonesia, my predecessor had been sent to a different country and I had to rebuild relationships with key partners. As the business structure was a production sharing agreement, every six months we negotiated work plans and budgets for the following period. As our capital burn rates were greater than $800 million per year, we had an entire multidisciplinary team composed of lawyers, accountants, relationship advisors, and engineers, meeting roughly the same match on the other side—in total about three dozen people on each side of the negotiation.

We'd get together in a hotel on the outskirts of town. A large meeting room would be laid out with four to six negotiation tables. We had to reach alignments on a variety of elements, making up our common investment decisions from assumptions on production efficiencies to buyers' delivery contracted volumes for the next period. I was the lead negotiator on our side for a total of six cycles over a period of four years. The meetings were held in the local Bahasa Indonesia language, and we couldn't leave the hotel until all matters associated with the next six months' plan were resolved. Often, we stayed for days.

I had no choice but to learn how to negotiate. While I'd negotiated agreements before (such as areas of mutual interests, development plans, and joint venture partnerships), with such accountability on my hands, I had to give it my best. During the second year, we reached an impasse, and I needed to call my boss and ask for his help. He responded, "You're the lead negotiator. I'm not coming into the room. Discreetly meet me for breakfast in the restaurant around the corner from the hotel and let's talk through it."

This was THE help I needed. I barely remember the details now, but that support gave me the wings (and confidence) I needed to successfully conclude the negotiation that day.

Another time, I was the chair of an infrastructure consortium that was operating with an agreement that had been written without considerations for some of the subsequent circumstances that arose. The team had concluded that we couldn't re-open the agreement, but after long hours in meeting rooms (and legal advice on all sides) we entered a "seek-to-understand" the other party's positioning. When I arrived, I received phone calls from the operations coordinator on duty in late hours or on weekends to inform me that one party in the system wasn't playing fair and was pushing the infrastructure design capacity near its limits. As a result, we had no choice but to take our products off to ease the load. Significant losses would be incurred on our side by doing so, but they knew we were put over a barrel and had no choice. It took months of "seeking to come to a shared understanding" and ultimately, we succeeded in negotiating (through a collaborative approach) a new standard operating procedure that's still in place today. We finally succeeded because we transparently shared data, stopped aggressively positioning and anchoring ourselves, and opened up to a different approach: leveraging the power of diversity.

Finding the right subject matter experts, seeking to understand both qualitatively and quantitatively the stance to help with the negotiation positioning, and above all coming at it by parking egos at the door with humility, are the winning ingredients to conclude any negotiation successfully. Leveraging the skill sets of the team members and their unique attributes is the ace in the hole that often gets overlooked, and as a result, teams will not make the progress and have the outcomes they desire. I know what I bring to a negotiation table, and I know when I'm not the best person to carry out the next steps and have learned to leverage my trusted allies. As an example, if you need to come in and grab it all with no intention of preserving any possibility of future engagements, I'm not your gal. On the other hand, if you need to negotiate successfully with a party with whom you will want to do enduring business, I might be the ace-in-the-hole you have. In negotiations, know thyself.

Chapter summary

In this chapter, I explore the distinctive traits and strategies employed by men and women negotiators through insights gained from an interview with Roger Greenfield, a renowned negotiator and partner at the GAP Partnership. The discussion highlights how understanding these differences, and harnessing the strengths of both genders, can lead to more effective and empowering negotiation outcomes.

Key takeaways and insights

Ego and competitive behavior: Men often perceive powerful women as threats, which can lead to more aggressive, power-based negotiation tactics. Women tend to favor collaboration and understanding, fostering more creative and mutually beneficial solutions.

1. **Collaboration and creativity**: Greenfield shares that a collaborative approach, often championed by women, reduces conflict and enhances successful outcomes. Women may have a propensity to collaborate, understand needs, and generate innovative solutions. Their ability to build trust and explore creative avenues is invaluable in negotiations. Men, on the other hand, may have a propensity to leverage certain aspects of the negotiations, such as gaining informal insights through trusted relationships, which can result in a significant advantage in finding creative solutions.

The best negotiators are those who can combine these approaches, revealing collective knowledge to achieve innovative solutions.

2. **Assertiveness and negotiation outcomes**: Men generally exhibit more assertiveness, helping them anchor negotiations in their favor. Women may be less assertive, which can impact their negotiation results, yet this is an area that has caused challenges for individuals in minority settings and should be employed carefully. Enhancing assertiveness in women, while maintaining their warm and collaborative strengths, is suggested to improve effectiveness.

Recognizing the need for assertiveness and framing proposals with objectivity can help everyone navigate tough negotiations with greater confidence.

3. **Confidence and counterproposals**: Men are often more confident and without hesitation will not accept the first offer instead, counter-proposing to secure better terms. Confidence is crucial for women in negotiations. Recent studies are showing that women feel more and more empowered to counter-propose and not settle for initial offers, yet there seem to be greater biases we don't fully understand at play when it comes to negotiation outcomes such as compensation. As a society, employers should continue to explore what inhibitors and disparity exist to achieve more equitable

compensation for all; our work is not done!

Practical steps, such as preparation, clarification, and problem-solving, can help everyone effectively frame their counterproposals and enhance their negotiation outcomes.

4. **Emotional intelligence**: Women typically have a better grasp of certain aspects of emotional intelligence, such as emotional self-awareness, interpersonal relationship, and empathy, which can be a powerful tool in influencing negotiations. In a business where men are a majority, they might understand the network in parties' interactions better, which can significantly enhance the negotiation approach.

Both men and women can benefit from cultivating emotional intelligence, using it to guide negotiations towards successful outcomes.

Conclusion

Considering the gender-specific traits and strategies in negotiations allows for the adoption of techniques that harness the best attributes of your negotiation team. By adopting a balanced approach that leverages collaboration, creativity, assertiveness, confidence, and emotional intelligence, negotiators can drive more successful and equitable results. Recognizing and cultivating these strengths, while also addressing potential biases, will empower negotiators to achieve their goals and build enduring relationships.

My Story

Love the people you work with and the people you live with even more

---

In my current role at Strategic Decisions Group, as a director on the board of various enterprises, and as the Chair for the Schulich School of Engineering Dean's Industry Advisory Council, I apply my experience to help clients and organizations navigate strategies and manage uncertainty and risk in their decision-making processes. This phase represents a renaissance of sorts—bringing new life to my career and leveraging my journey to benefit others. I focus on fostering innovation, strategic growth, and inclusion insights across various industries. This is a time for me to share and explore solutions for others purposefully, using my perspective and experiences to create positive change. What better way than to venture into authorship to reach beyond borders?

But what was the route I took to get here and what are the transformations, milestones, and epiphanies I met on the way? I grew up in a medium-sized city in the north of eastern Canada, surrounded by water, lakes, rivers, forests, and nature, far away from skyscrapers. My leadership abilities were identified when, at a young age, I led many activities while attending a summer camp. At the end of the two weeks, the camp leaders approached my parents and me, asking if I'd join their association council. This work involved constructs of governance, policies, and administrative skills. I developed a significant sense of responsibility and accountability for the success of the organization and attended strategic planning meetings. I wasn't even a teenager then, but it was the start of my journey as a leader.

In my professional career, I went on to achieve senior leadership levels, including vice-presidency in multinational corporations. I am a woman of STEM (science, technology, engineering, and mathematics) and made a career out of it: carving my way through, in some cases, chiseling the tunnels in hard rock. In many instances, I didn't know if I'd ever see the light at the end of the tunnel.

I've done it all, leading large organizations, being one of a few women in my country who could say they managed billion-dollar portfolios over many years, and more recently, offering business consulting and serving on boards.

But let's go back to the beginning.

In my school life, my friends were evenly split when it came to gender, and the commonality we had was we were interested in helping each other think and learn. I played badminton competitively in my province and spent my evenings and weekends modeling for well-known designers. My modeling years equipped me with the skills to navigate many future situations. In particular, we were trained and taught how to adapt to the environment and blend in in a way that would highlight the designer (not us), yet we were ambassadors for the strategy (product, marketing, representation). We also learned how to introduce ourselves in any social circle. I became great at understanding what to observe in the environments I was put in—the habits, culture, rites and customs.

When it came to my college years, I remember going to the career counselor and asking what I should pursue at university. He said, "Answer this list of over a hundred multiple-choice questions about your likes, dislikes, passions, and motivators. I'll combine this with your marks to give us a full picture, then let's look at the results together." I did that and sat opposite the counselor at his desk afterward, reflecting on this relatively Cartesian method.

"You fit a mechanical engineering profile," he said.

"Are there jobs in that field?"

"Absolutely there are."

He provided me with some stats on employment rates. To the surprise of my family, I'd picked my calling: to become a mechanical engineer. I'm lucky, because my parents, along with my sister and now deceased brother, have been a constant and solid empowering force in my life, and their unwavering support enabled me to pursue my passions.

I envisioned a stable career within Quebec's industrial landscape, surrounded by family and friends, in a world where I knew my place and the path ahead seemed clear. This wasn't going to be my future. In fact, the following summer I left the region never to return except for brief family visits.

The first few years of university weren't a walk in the park; if you started with a class of roughly two hundred, there were one hundred left by the end of the first year and fifty by the end of the second. Then you chose your discipline (mine had already been chosen as mechanical) and you had a fair chance of graduating at the end of your four years of undergrad. There was roughly 9% women in my mechanical engineering graduating class.

Because of my summer jobs while I was in university working as a process plant operator then as an engineering student the following year to design a nodal analysis model, I was the first in my graduating class to find a full-time job.

In my early career days, I was navigating this male dominated-world using a trial-and-error approach, fitting in in some circumstances and being an outcast in others. I had some of my best relationships with an operations foreman at the time and one of my worst with another. At one point, while working on a compressor installation on a remote site, a worker asked me, "What's a woman doing in this environment?"

I fumbled for an answer back then, but I wish I could go back to that lunchroom conversation and say, "I do exactly like all the other people in my role; I just happen not to have the same body type and yes, I'm a little spirited, courageous, and have a bold trait or two!"

I worked with a medium-sized firm founded by Jim Gray, a phenomenal gentleman and inspiring leader with whom I stay in touch even to this day. I was very lucky to work for such a value-based organization at the start of my career. It was a technical excellence-oriented organization, which made it much easier on the gender inclusion side. Because of the high competency of the staff, a sense of mutual respect for what we brought to the company was shared and transpired in all our work interactions. I made the closest friends of my career there, although at the time I didn't know it was so special! I realized after the fact this sense of teamwork, agnostic to gender, wasn't the norm in our industry. We were really winning together. We had great appreciation for everyone's contributions from Don the head negotiator, and Denise in geology, to Dean in the mail room. We had a sense of belonging fostered in part by our benevolent fundraising for the United Way, for which we were a star company many years in a row. We achieved 100% contribution during the yearly campaign and brought more high impact Leadership Donors than an array of active multinationals with many more employees. We had a sense we could do anything together if we put our minds to it. This closeness and bond we shared was reaffirmed as recently as two years ago. The company ceased to exist in the late nineties and more than forty people showed up to welcome me back in town after I'd taken an assignment away for four years. Just last year, twenty-five years after the sale of the company, a reunion brought hundreds of people together from all parts of the continent.

The first few years of my career were focused on being a sponge and learning to build competency as much as I could. In fact, I started building a binder of knowledge of all the things I'd mastered enough to teach someone, capturing the equations and notes on each concept, and organizing them in alphabetical order. In later years, I recommended adopting a similar "binder of knowledge approach" to mentees, because engineering (like many fields) is broad, and you learn a lot by being assigned specific projects. Furthermore, building a knowledge collection is a nice way to own your craft and know what you know. Such a practice will have proven to be one of the gap bridging elements of my career: a focus on competency.

There are a few turning points in my history that transformed my world. The salient ones are attributed with *aha!* moments that came my way often from unexpected places. They range from the day I realized I couldn't emulate my male counterparts and succeed using the same leadership traits to the day I decided to negotiate my way back into budgetary accountabilities. My focus was (to use a backcountry skiing analogy) to break trail for others. As I was breaking trail, I realized that to enable ALL to reach their full potential and maximize their contribution to the prosperity of our society, we need to help, engage, and enlist EVERYONE on the journey (women and men). This simple yet also complex realization came to me in a conversation with my dear friend Ian over dinner on a vacation night in Mexico. It was crystal clear: we wouldn't win in inclusion and would continue to leave so much potential in the sidelines if we only focused on trying to resolve women's barriers to success. We needed to enable everyone and transform our rapport with each other.

As I navigated through my career, I faced numerous tests, venturing in many less than common pathways. For example, I took the helicopter underwater escape training (HUET) to be able to work offshore. Few women take this training, and I was tremendously grateful to know at least one who'd done it before to lean on. At a high level, this training involves getting into a cage resembling the fuselage of a helicopter, buckling yourself up in a seatbelt, and getting dunked in a body of water (usually an indoor pool) and having to escape. This is a repeat experience where you're in a controlled environment to test your abilities and gain the confidence to do it successfully should you experience a helicopter crash over water. They don't let you go until you've proven you can do it on your own (at least three times out of five).

Of all the tests in my career, this one required the most courage, perhaps along with confined space firefighting training; even more than media and public speaking, which is never a walk in the park. Along my non-traditional journey, I've appreciated having experienced people of the same gender as I worked through my fears. I've also appreciated taking my own turn in helping others, such as the time a lady failed her first HUET attempt and was sobbing in the shower room.

Each new role brought its own set of technical challenges and learning opportunities. However, I also found allies—colleagues, mentors, and industry leaders who believed in me, removed barriers for me, and supported my journey. Together, we overcame obstacles and celebrated successes.

A woman who worked in a non-traditional field herself, my official career mentor Janice, became the one

I phoned (regardless of where I was in the world) if I had a major decision to make. As she's also a mom, she even gave me sage advice on motherhood.

When I first met Janice, I naively thought I was going to be treated like the men at work. After all, why not? I had the same education and had held some of the best development roles amongst my peers. I soon saw the world wasn't equal, and it wasn't made for women to feel at home. I was sad that some of my female colleagues, who were smarter than me, stopped working to care for their kids and never returned to their careers. I didn't know how to help the downward trend, though I knew we were leaving so much on the table by not harvesting the fruit of this investment in the form of training and education for the bright minds of our society. I couldn't understand that despite my best efforts, what was at play was what has recently been coined for individuals in minority settings as *microaggressions*. These subtle but impactful experiences accumulate and often become too much, resulting in many abandoning their calling.

As for me, I continued to march along and was assigned various international roles. In many of these I was a *multifer*—I embodied multiple aspects of diversity. I didn't grow up with the same first language as my coworkers, didn't have the same racial heritage, and wasn't of the same gender. The ultimate experience was the few days I spent in the middle of the West Natuna Sea, on a platform with sixty-five Indonesian men. My fluency in Bahasa Indonesia, the language in the dinner hall, was basic. I was the only woman there, and they had to allocate one of the washrooms in the working area to me. At night, I slept in the room adjacent to the offshore facilities on-duty doctor, and the room was equipped with a shared jack-and-jill bathroom.

At first, I felt like a fish out of water, but with courage and curiosity, ultimately, the visit was an absolute success. We discussed, amongst other things, strategies to deal with operational issues. We took a day trip to an adjacent floating storage unit. Finally, someone was celebrating their twentieth work anniversary that week, so we shared a phenomenal extra spicy freshly caught fish and sang karaoke in the evening. What made me smile the most was their morning rituals, inspired by police training, where they did a five-to-ten-minute stretch together in the lunch hall right after breakfast before starting their day, which of course I was delighted to partake in.

During my four years in Asia, I started sending pictures back home to my sister with the instruction to *find the one that's different from the others*. There's a particularly striking photograph where eleven of us are wearing full personal protective equipment, including the same color coveralls, with me alone with ten gentlemen. This phase of my journey was about applying what I'd learned to make a positive impact on my ecosystem. I was on a mission to demystify the presence of women in this operational world, with the hopes that with less discomfort would come more openness for all. I also led large engineering technical teams of several hundred people from all specialities: electrical, mechanical, chemical, civil, naval, etc. Throughout my career, I was focused on fostering a culture of innovation, collaboration, and diversity, ensuring the environment I was in benefited from a broad range of perspectives and talents and that to the best extent possible, it welcomed inclusivity.

With a long career as a woman in non-traditional fields, not just in North America but internationally, what I bring back in my toolkit is multifaceted—knowledge, experience, and a deep commitment to inclusion and diversity. With participation in such initiatives as Mentor Walks, I work to dismantle barriers and create opportunities for the next generation. By sharing my journey from a remote francophone region to the global stage and everything in between, my hope is to inspire others, no matter how unconventional their paths may be.

This is my true essence—transforming challenges into opportunities and using my experiences to pave the way for future trailblazers. Each step forward is a testament to the resilience and the power of diverse perspectives. I appreciate the gentlemen in my current environment who are having fun working with women and value our contribution authentically. I appreciate the gentlewomen in my environment who are challenging the status quo authentically. It takes accepting some discomfort to reach sustained new heights together. Just this week, I was in a board meeting and realized how phenomenal it was to be in a gender-balanced group (achieved because of our intentional succession planning and recruitment). It made my heart full to be surrounded by a smart and strategic group of people working together in mutual respect.

Please consider being daring with me. Dare to venture beyond the ordinary, proving that with the right support and mindset, the extraordinary is within reach and in all of us.

Afterword

Celebrating Diversity and Individual Achievements

What then is truth? A movable host of metaphors, metonyms, and anthropomorphisms: in short, a sum of human relations which have been poetically and rhetorically intensified, transferred, and embellished, and which, after long use, seem firm, canonical, and obligatory to a people: truths are illusions about which one has forgotten that this is what they are; metaphors which are worn out and without sensuous power; coins which have lost their pictures and now matter only as metal, no longer as coins.

Friedrich Nietzsche[80]

We've had quite an exploratory journey in harnessing the power of US; imagining, and rethinking our world beyond traditional roles. AND YET, AND YET it's a stark reality today that we have a journey ahead and we're still leaving money on the table (figuratively and practically speaking). We're evolving together, and it will take all of us, active and aware of the possibilities in our respective ecosystems, to continue to break through. Specifically, we need to activate a magic spark to create a collective momentum and go further. The power, and societal value that will come from advancing everyone's ability to pursue their careers and passions, and at the same time thrive in their home lives regardless of gender is beyond significant. We could try to quantify it, but deep down we know that the happiness, self-worth and prosperity that comes from knowing that you've proudly pursued a fulfilling career and passion while sustaining an extraordinary life at home with your life partner and family is beyond compare.

By embracing your masculine or feminine energy at home and doubling down on the superpowers of your archetype at work, you'll inevitably grow and positively transform your entire ecosystem with impacts far reaching beyond your expectations.

We must celebrate our wins together too, as this work is hard and the path is circuitous. We won't be able to build on the momentum we create without intentionally acknowledging and celebrating it along the way. We also need to continue to share our experiences and what worked well in the integration of diversity in our different cultures. How bringing various backgrounds and perspectives has helped us. We ought to celebrate and promote allies and advocates of those paving the way for others to come after them. Celebrations give wings to those with the courage to pursue paths less travelled, daring to be architects of a dazzling shared future.

We also need to celebrate our career milestones, our personal growth moments, our achievements when we open new doors. This is the only way we'll overcome inertia and make long-lasting progress.

What will be the next thing we'll celebrate together? Drop me a note on my Instagram at **usandyet** to let me know. I'd love to hear.

When I first started writing, I thought we needed to establish peer groups to share and support each other. It turns out these groups already exist; they're called *Lean In*. It is important that the diversity profile of these groups become more and more representative of society because this is the only way we'll be able to capture our potential; this is about us RISING TOGETHER BEYOND TRADITIONAL ROLES and thriving.

Over to you...

Let's get inspired!

Follow the QR code for more ideas and tools or just to let me know you're IN on the journey to build this extraordinary, diverse, and equitable future.

www.usandyet.com

References

[1] Walter Wriston, *AZQuotes.com*, Wind and Fly LTD, 2024. https://www.azquotes.com/quote/748229 [accessed July 25, 2024.]

[2] AltoPartners, "International Women's Day 2024: Unlocking the 172 trillion gender dividend" (2024), https://altopartners.com/news/2024-international-womens-day-2024-unlocking-the-usd-172-trillion-gender-dividend [accessed May 6, 2024].

[3] Quentin Wodon, Adenike Onagoruwa, Chata Malé, Claudio Montenegro, Hoa Nguyen, and Bénédicte de la Brière, "How large is the gender dividend? Measuring the impacts and costs of gender inequality" (2020), World Bank Publications—Reports 33396, The World Bank Group https://documents.worldbank.org/en/publication/documents-reports [accessed May 6, 2024].

[4] Wodon et al., "How large is the gender dividend?" p. 23.

[5] Kim S. Cameron, Positive Leadership – Strategies for Extraordinary Performance (Berrett-Koehler Publishers, 2008), p. 22.

[6] Michael McKinney, "Leadership Now – Building A community of Leaders," https://www.leadershipnow.com/about.html, *Leading Blog* (2008) [July 25, 2024].

[7] McKinney, "Building A community of Leaders."

[8] Barbara L. Fredrickson, "The Role of Positive Emotions in Positive Psychology- The Broaden-and-Build Theory of Positive Emotions", *University of Michigan American Psychologist,* March 2001, p.218.

[9] McKinsey & Company and LeanIn, "Diversity Wins: How Inclusion Matters." (2020). https://www.mckinsey.com/featured-insights/diversity-and-inclusion/diversity-wins-how-inclusion-matters [accessed July 26, 2024].

[10] Qantas, Shaping our future Quantas annual report 2014, https://investor.qantas.com/FormBuilder/_Resource/_module/doLLG5ufYkCyEPjF1tpgyw/file/annual-reports/2014AnnualReport.pdf [accessed July 26, 2024].

[11] Juliet Bourke and Bernadette Dillon, "The diversity and inclusion revolution—eight powerful truths", *Deloitte Review*, issue 22, p. 83.

[12] AltoPartners, "International Women's Day 2024: Unlocking the 172 trillion gender dividend," (2024). https://altopartners.com/news/2024-international-women-s-day-2024-unlocking-the-usd-172-trillion-gender-dividend [accessed July 26, 2024].

[13] ABM Fazle Rahi. "Unpacking women's power on corporate boards: gender reward
in board composition," *International Journal of Disclosure and Governance* (2024). https://link.springer.com/article/10.1057/s41310-024-00228-5 [accessed July 26, 2024].

[14] The Global Compact. "Who Cares Wins. Connecting Financial Markets to a Changing World. Recommendations by the financial industry to better integrate environmental, social and governance issues in analysis, asset management and securities brokerage" (2004), https://www.unepfi.org/fileadmin/events/2004/stocks/who

_cares_wins_global_compact_2004.pdf [accessed July 26, 2024].

[15] David F. Larcker and Tjomme O. Rusticus, "On the use of instrumental variables in accounting research," *Journal of Accounting and Economics,* volume 49, issue 3, April 2010, pp. 186–205, https://www.sciencedirect.com/science/article/abs/pii/S0165410109000718 [accessed July 26, 2024].

[16] ABM Fazle Rahi, "Unpacking women's power on corporate boards: gender reward in board composition", *International Journal of Disclosure and Governance* (2024), p. 2.

[17] Juliet Bourke and Bernadette Dillon, "The diversity and inclusion revolution: Eight powerful truths," *Deloitte Review*, issue 22, January 2018, https://internationalwim.org/iwim-reports/the-diversity-and-inclusion-revolution-eight-powerful-truths/ [accessed July 26, 2024].

[18] Juliet Bourke, Which two heads are better than one? How diverse teams create breakthrough ideas and make smarter decisions (Australian Institute of Company Directors, 2016).

[19] Helen Wilkinson, *No Turning Back – Generations and the Genderquake* (Demos Papers, 1994).

[20] Eckhart Tolle, Oneness With All Life: Inspirational Selections from A New Earth (Penguin, 2008), p. 50.

[21] Wilkinson, *No Turning Back*, pp.60-67

[22] P. Kajonius and J. Johnson, "Sex differences in 30 facets of the five factor model of personality in the large public (N = 320,128)," *Personality and Individual Differences*, vol. 129, 15 July 2018, pp. 126–130; S. Whyte; R. Brooks; H. Chan and B Torgler, "Sex differences in sexual attraction for aesthetics, resources and personality across age," *PLoS ONE*, 2021.

[23] Thomas Eckes and Hanns Martin Trautner, *The Developmental Social Psychology of Gender* (Psychology Press, 2000), p. 296.
[24] Nuala G. Walsh, "Perfectionism: Escaping the Perfectionist Trap: 7 signs and 7 solutions," *Psychology Today,* 30 June 2023, https://www.psychologytoday.com/gb/blog/decisions-that-matter/202306/escaping-the-perfectionist-trap-7-signs-and-7-solutions [accessed July 26, 2024].
[25] Tony Robbins, *I am not your guru*, 2016 documentary, www.netflix.com. You can view the session we attended in this documentary-at one point you can even see us in the audience!
[26] US bureau of labor statistics, https://www.bls.gov/cps/cpsaat11.htm "Plant Operator Demographics and Statistics in the US" (2021), *Zippia*, https://www.zippia.com/power-plant-operator-jobs/demographics/ [accessed July 26, 2024].
[27] Clara Plückelmann, Marie Gustafsson, Claudia Bernhard-Oettel, Constanze Leineweber, and Sabine Sczesny, "Women's and men's experiences with participative decision-making at workplace and organizational levels", *Frontiers in Psychology,* volume 14, 2023, p. 1.
[28] "Bloomberg Media Unveils New Look for Bloomberg Pursuits Magazine," *Bloomberg Press,* (2015), July 23, 2024.
[29] EngineeringUK–Inspiring Futures Together, *From A level to Engineering- Exploring the gender gap in higher education,* www.engineeringUK.com/alevels, [May 16, 2024]
[30] Su Maddock, Challenging Women – gender, culture and organization (Sage Publications, 1999).
[31] Raden Adjeng Kartini, *Letters of a Javanese Princess* (London: Dickworth and Co., 1921), https://www.gutenberg.org/files/34647/34647-h/34647-h.htm [accessed July 26, 2024].

[32] Esteban Ortiz-Ospina and Max Roser, "Marriages and Divorces," *Our World in Data*, https://ourworldindata.org/marriages-and-divorces, first published July 2020 and revised April 2024 [accessed July 25, 2024].

[33] Marie F. Mongan M. Ed. M.Hy., Eliza Foss, et al, HypnoBirthing: The Mongan Method: A Natural Approach to Safer, Easier, More Comfortable Birthing, (Souvenir Press, 2015).

[34] Brigitte Sumner, Give him back his balls – For happy relationships (MyVoice Publishing, 2007).

[35] Sumner, Give him back his balls, p. 19.

[36] World Economic Forum. "Global Gender Gap Report 2023" https://www.nedaglobal.com/ned-insights/news/wef-global-gender-gap-report-2023/#nogo [accessed July 30, 2024].

[37] Katherine Haan, "Gender Pay Gap Statistics in 2024," *Forbes Advisor*, 2024, https://www.forbes.com/advisor/business/gender-pay-gap-statistics [accessed July 30, 2024].

[38] AAUW.org Workplace & Economic Equity, "Fast Facts: The Gender Pay Gap," https://www.aauw.org/resources/article/fast-facts-pay-gap/ [accessed July 26, 2024]

[39] Sam Jones, "Spain hopes domestic tasks app will ensure men pull their weight," *Guardian*, May 19, 2023, https://www.theguardian.com/world/2023/may/19/spain-domestic-tasks-app-chores-family-members [accessed July 30, 2024].

[40] Kate Mangino, Equal Partners—Improving Gender Equality at Home (St. Martin's Press, 2022).

[41] Emine Saner, "The woman's to-do list is relentless: how to achieve an equal split of household chores," *Guardian*, August 15, 2022,

https://www.theguardian.com/money/2022/aug/15/how-to-achieve-an-equal-split-of-household-chores-kate-mangino [accessed July 30, 2024].

[42] Tim Brown, "Design Thinking," *Harvard Business Review*, 2008, https://hbr.org/2008/06/design-thinking [accessed July 30, 2024].

[43] Esther Han, "What Is Design Thinking & Why Is It Important?" *Harvard Business School Online*, January 18, 2022, https://online.hbs.edu/blog/post/what-is-design-thinking [accessed July 30, 2024].

[44] McKinsey & Company, "What is psychological safety?" July 17, 2023, https://www.mckinsey.com/featured-insights/mckinsey-explainers/what-is-psychological-safety [accessed July 30, 2024].

[45] McKinsey & Company, "What is psychological safety?"

[46] Free translation from French. Jacques Languirand, "Observatoire de la Philthérapie", Article #35- La lumiere entre par les failles. (June 2024)

[47] Jason L Arthur, Male Vs Female Driving Statistics [2024]: Who's Safer? (LookupAplate, January 12, 2024), https://www.lookupaplate.com/blog/men-vs-female-driving-statistics/ [accessed May 20, 2024].

[48] Alina Florentina Burlacu and Karla Conzalez Carvajal, "Who is safer on the road, men or women?" *World Bank Blogs*, March 3, 2021, https://blogs.worldbank.org/en/transport/who-safer-road-men-or-women [accessed May 20, 2024]

[49] Burlacu and Conzalez Carvajal, "Who is safer on the road, men or women?"

[50] Bruckheim and Patel, "Male vs Female Driving Statistics", *Brukcheim & Patel*, www.brucklaw.com, October 13, 2022, [accessed May 20, 2024] [

[51] Giovanna Coi, "Men and their cars: Cities aim to break up the love affair", POLITICO, Living Cities, October 5, 2022), [accessed May 20, 2024]

[52] Jason L. Arthur, "Male Vs Female Driving Statistics [2024]: Who's Safer?" (*LookupAplate,* January 12, 2024), https://www.lookupaplate.com/blog/men-vs-female-driving-statistics/ [accessed May 20, 2024].

[53] Arthur, "Male Vs Female Driving Statistics."

[54] International Bank for Reconstruction and Development, HANDBOOK for Gender-Inclusive Urban Planning Design", *The World Bank*, 2020, https://documents1.worldbank.org/curated/en/363451579616767708/pdf/Handbook-for-Gender-Inclusive-Urban-Planning-and-Design.pdf.

[55] Jack Zenger and Joseph Folkman, "Women Are Better Leaders During a Crisis," *Harvard Business Review,* December 30, 2020, https://hbr.org/2020/12/research-women-are-better-leaders-during-a-crisis [accessed July 30, 2024].

[56] Su Maddock, Challenging Women – gender, culture and organization (Sage Publications, 1999), p.9.

[57] Nicole Murphy, "Types of Bias" *CPD Online College*, https://cpdonline.co.uk/knowledge-base/safeguarding/types-of-bias/ November 2021 [July 29, 2024]

[58] "Why So Few 'Diversity' Candidates Are Hired," *Harvard Business Publishing,* https://www.harvardbusiness.org/insight/why-so-few-diversity-candidates-are-hired/ [accessed July 30, 2024].

[59] Stefanie K. Johnson, David R Hekman, and Elsa T. Chan, "If there's Only One Woman in Your Candidate Pool, There's Statistically No Chance She'll Be Hired," *Harvard Business Review,* April 26, 2016, https://hbr.org/2016/04/if-theres-only-one-woman-in-your-candidate-pool-theres-

statistically-no-chance-shell-be-hired [accessed July 30, 2024].
[60] Erika Ryan, Courtney Dorning, Ari Shapiro, "Powerful women tend to be called by their first name. It's not an accident", *NPR- culture,* https://www.npr.org/2024/07/24/nx-s1-5049773/powerful-women-tend-to-be-called-by-their-first-name-its-not-an-accident, July 24, 2024 [accessed Aug 27, 2024].
[61] Isha, Inner Engineering. www.Isha.sadhguru.org [accessed July 29, 2024].
[62] Denise-Marie Ordway. "Economics, Education, Health, Race & Gender- What research says about the kids of working moms." [Overall, maternal employment seems to have a limited impact on children's behavior and academic achievement over the short term. And there appear to be benefits in the long-term. A study published in 2018 finds that daughters raised by working moms are more likely to be employed as adults and have higher incomes]. *The Journalist's Resource, Informing the news* (August 6, 2018) p. 2.
[63] Julie Garland-McLellan, "International Women's Day 2024: Unlocking the 172 trillion gender dividend," *AltoPartners, Executive Search & Leadership Advisory* (2024), p.18.
[64] Helen Wilkinson, No Turning Back – Generations and the Genderquake (Demos Papers, 1994), p. 28.
[65] Scott Coltrane, "Research on Household Labor: Modeling and Measuring Social Embeddedness of Routine Family Work," *Journal of Marriage and Family,* 62, no. 4 (2000): 1208-1233.
[66] Lynn Price Cook, "'Doing' Gender in Context: Household Bargaining and Risk of Divorce in Germany and the United States," *American Journal of Sociology* 112, no. 2 (2006). 442-72.

[67] Eunice Kennedy Shriver, "*Findings for Children up to Age 4½ Years*", National Institute of Child Health and Human Development, (2006).

[68] Eunice Kennedy Shriver, "*Findings for Children up to Age 4½ years*", National Institute of Child Health and Human Development Early Child Care Research Network, "Fathers' and Mothers' Parenting Behavior and Beliefs as Predictors of Children's Social Adjustment and Transition to School," *Journal of Family Psychology*. 18, no. 4 (2004); 628-38) and National Institute of Child Health and Human Development, "Child-Care Effect Sizes," p. 113.

[69] Kathleen L. McGinn, Mayra Ruiz Castro, and Elizabeth Long Lingo. "Learning From Mum: Cross-National Evidence Linking Maternal Employment and Adult Children's Outcomes." Work, Employment and Society 33, no. 3 (June 2019): 374–400.

[70] A physical board in the https://hotyogaon17th.com/ studio.

[71] David R. Hawkins M.D. Ph.D., *Power vs. Force: The Hidden Determinants of Human Behavior*, (Hay House LLC, 2014). p. 154.

[72] UN Women, Gender Equality Accelerators. *UN Women*, https://www.unwomen.org/en/what-we-do/gender-equality-accelerators (2023) [accessed May 30, 2024]

[73] UN Women, In focus: Sustainable Development Goal 5- Achieving gender equality and empowering all women and girls. *UN Women*, https://www.unwomen.org/en/news-stories/in-focus/2022/08/in-focus-sustainable-development-goal-5 (August 23, 2022) [accessed May 30, 2024]

[74] Katie O'Malley, "Leonard Cohen: Most Iconic Quotes- Poet. Singer. Songwriter. Following the death of Leonard Cohen, we look back at his most profound sentiments.", *Elle- Life-*

Culture https://www.elle.com/uk/life-and-culture/culture, p. 9.

[75] Devon Denomme, Jennifer Lombardo, Wendy Kwong, "Negotiation | Definition, Process & Stages", *Study.com*, https://study.com/academy/lesson/what-is-negotiation-the-five-steps-of-the-negotiation-process.html. [accessed August 28, 2024].

[76] Maryam Meschkat and Reza Nejati, "Does Emotional Intelligence Depend on Gender? A Study on Undergraduate English Majors of Three Iranian Universities", *SAGE Open* July-September 2017: 1–8, p. 1.

[77] Harvard DCE Professional & Executive Development, "How to Improve Your Emotional Intelligence," Harvard Division of Continuing Education, https://professional.dce.harvard.edu/blog/how-to-improve-your-emotional-intelligence/, August 26, 2019 [accessed August 28, 2024]

[78] Laura J. Kray, Jessica A. Kennedy, and Margaret Lee, "Now, Women Do Ask: A Call to Update Beliefs about the Gender Pay Gap," *Academy of Management Discoveries* VOL. 10, NO. 1., March 28, 2024, p.1.

[79] Kim Elsesser, "Women More Likely To Negotiate Salaries But Still Earn Less Than Men, Research Says", *Forbes Leadership Careers*, https://www.forbes.com/sites/kimelsesser/2023/11/02/women-more-likely-to-negotiate-salaries-but-still-earn-less-than-men-research-says/, November 2, 2023, [accessed August 29, 2024]

[80] Friedrich Nietzsche and Tim Newcomb. *On Truth and Lies in an Extra-Moral Sense* ("Über Wahrheit und Lüge im außermoralischen Sinne"), (2019) p.6.

www.ingramcontent.com/pod-product-compliance
Lightning Source LLC
Chambersburg PA
CBHW030436010526
44118CB00011B/669